Religion, Democracy and Israeli Society

The Sherman Lecture Series

The Sherman Lecture Series is an annual series supported by the Sherman Trust on behalf of the School of Oriental and African Studies, London, UK.

Edited by Dr Tudor Parfitt and Professor John Hinnels, School of Oriental and African Studies, London, UK.

Volume 1   *Sephardi Religious Responses to Modernity*
             Norman A. Stillman
Volume 2   *Religion, Democracy and Israeli Society*
             Charles S. Liebman

ISSN 1023-7917

Religion, Democracy and Israeli Society

Charles S. Liebman

Bar-Ilan University, Israel

LONDON AND NEW YORK

First published in 1997 by Overseas Publishers Association

Published 2006 by Routledge
2 Park Square, Milton Park, Abingdon, Oxfordshire OX14 4RN
711 Third Avenue, New York, NY 10017

First issued in paperback 2016

Routledge is an imprint of the Taylor and Francis Group, an informa business

Copyright © 1997 OPA (Overseas Publishers Association)
Amsterdam B.V.

British Library Cataloguing in Publication Data

Liebman, Charles S.
  Religion, democracy and Israeli society. – (The Sherman
  Lecture series ; 2)
  1. Religion and politics – Israel   2. Religious fundamentalism
  – Israel   3. Religion and sociology – Israel
  I. Title
  291.1'77'095694

ISBN 13: 978-1-138-98505-6 (pbk)
ISBN 13: 978-90-5702-012-4 (hbk)

Publisher's Note
The publisher has gone to great lengths to ensure the quality of this reprint but points out that some imperfections in the original may be apparent

To Larry Kobrin for his friendship

And the Patrons of the Yehuda Avner Chair in Religion and Politics at Bar-Ilan University for their support.

Helen and Maurice Alter
Gini and Hans Bachrach
Eva and Marc Besen
Elaine Bloch-Jaffe
Gerda and Joseph Brender
Yvonne Fink
Harry Flicker
Pauline and John Gandel
Stera and Rabbi Joseph Gutnick
Eddie Kornhauser
Seyma Lederman
Naomi and Isi Leibler
Rosanna and Mark Leibler
Rosie and Solomon Lew
The Liberman Family
Minya and Leon Lipkies
Minnie and David Mandie
Lisa and Levi Mochkin
Nechama and Nathan Werdiger
Della and Fred Worms

Contents

Preface

The essays in this volume are revisions, in some cases substantial, to the 1995 Sherman Lectures which I delivered at SOAS, the School of Oriental and African Studies of the University of London. I am very grateful to John Hinnells, chairman of the Religion Department at SOAS and to Tudor Parfitt, director of its Center for Judaic Studies who issued the invitation to me and co-sponsored the lectures. I am additionally grateful for the hospitality which they offered me while I was in London, they both went out of their way to make my stay enjoyable. I would like to think that my association with both these erudite and charming people is the beginning of a continued association and a lasting friendship.

I found the audience for the Sherman lectures to be remarkably knowledgeable and astute. They offered a number of very keen observations which I am pleased to incorporate in the revised lectures that constitute the present volume.

The introductory chapter is an expansion of some remarks which I offered at the opening of my first lecture. It is an effort to map out the field of religion and politics. An increasing number of scholars have been writing in the field of religion and politics but to the best of my knowledge no one has attempted to delineate the field or identify its boundaries. I do not pretend that my introductory remarks can substitute for the kind of rigorous essay that the subject matter demands.

The remaining chapters cover certain aspects or touch certain small points on the large map which I outline in that introductory chapter. Religion and politics among Israeli Jews is the case study but I try, throughout the essays, to keep track of my major goal — illuminating the general topic of religion and politics.

Asher Cohen's name appears as the co-author of two chapters. It may seem strange to list a co-author of chapters that build on my own public lectures. However, chapter two is based on Cohen's recently completed doctoral dissertation. Furthermore, Cohen read that lecture, which is really a popularization of his dissertation, and in the course of doing so he made corrections and added further comments. Finally, he compiled the footnotes. It is only fair, therefore, that he appear as senior author of that chapter. He collaborated in preparing Chapter three. I want to thank the Yehuda Avner Chair in Religion and Politics at Bar-Ilan University for defraying the expenses incurred in preparing this book.

ONE

Introduction to the Field of Religion and Politics

What does "religion and politics" mean? I will argue that it is a field of study whose parameters are only beginning to be established. Methodologically, it means studies which utilize concepts, modes of thought and tools of analysis from both the field of politics and the field of religion. In this essay, however, I want to describe the substance rather than the methodology of the field. Many examples pertain to Judaism in Israel and, where possible, I have used illustrations that are relevant to the succeeding four chapters.

First of all, religion and politics deals with socio-political issues related to religion and the organizations, political parties and interest groups concerned with these issues. Religious parties and interest groups are the most widely studied aspect of religion and politics. In many countries, religious adherents organize political parties and/or political interest groups to pursue their interests in the public realm; sometimes in defense of their own community, sometimes in the imposition of religious values on the total society, often for both purposes. But this kind of religious involvement in politics is basically no different than the involvement of any other party or interest group. However, once the political institutions are in place, they are likely to develop their own interests and legitimate them in religious terms. For example, a religious party may raise demands which can not be explained in terms of religious values or the needs of the religious population which the organization serves but can best be understood in terms of the organization's own needs. The organization, however, is likely to claim that its demands are legitimate because it is defending religion or a religious community. This may be reprehensible but it is surely natural. Non-religious parties do the same sort of thing and rely on arguments for freedom or national interest or some other popular value to legitimate their claims.

It is true that the very act of participation in the political arena influences religion to some extent. For example, political participation promotes a new religious elite. One consequence of mobilizing religious constituencies for political purposes and representing these constituencies in the political arena is to add status and power to political rather than spiritual leaders within the religious establishment. But the standard tools of political analysis are quite adequate in helping us understand "religious" behavior of this sort.

A more interesting and subtle question falling under the rubric of socio-political issues is how religion, viewed as an aspect of culture, influences the broader political culture and public policy. This leads to the reverse question; how does political culture and public policy influence religion?

In addition to questions of a socio-political nature, the topic of religion and politics covers questions in the philosophical or normative realm. How does religion, which claims, at least in the Jewish and Muslim traditions, but in many respects in the Christian tradition as well, to cover all aspects of life, leave room for an independent polity and for the formation of public policy which is religiously neutral; and should religion, from its own perspective, leave room for a religiously neutral or independent polity if it has the power to prevent it? And if religion is not neutral with regard to public policy or the nature of the state, what sort of polity does religion envision? The reverse question, which is the more realistic one in western societies, is whether the political system which to seeks to establish a just and orderly society ought to leave a space, within the body politic, for religion, or can an orderly state only survive if religion is held to be an entirely private matter? And if the state refuses to leave a space for religion in the public order, can it

be a fair and/or an orderly society. I want to look at some of
these issues in more detail.

RELIGION AS A SOURCE OF POLITICAL CULTURE

Political culture is the set of moods, beliefs, assumptions, and
norms within which political activity takes place. It is the frame
for politics in any society. Religion shapes political culture
through its ideas or beliefs, its images and its structure.

Religious Ideas or Beliefs

Religions influence political culture by articulating their notions
about good and evil or right and wrong. For example, the
Catholic Church is opposed to abortions. The Church asserts that
the fetus should be treated as the equivalent of a human being
while it is in the mother's womb. The Muslim religion affirms
that consuming alcohol or eating pig meat is prohibited and
Judaism prohibits many types of activity on the Sabbath. This
has led Catholics to oppose legalizing abortions, Muslims to
demand the prohibition of sales of alcoholic drinks in countries
where they constitute a majority and religious Jews to insist that
movie theaters should be closed on the Sabbath in Israel. These
are examples of religious ideas directly effecting politics. But the
connection is not as simple as it may appear. First of all, there
are some serious Catholics, Muslims and Jews who believe that
something is sinful, even forbidden by God, without necessarily
believing that the state ought to prohibit it. They may feel that
sinful behavior should be prevented by educating the public,
and/or that it is best left for the individual to decide for himself
how to behave and punishment of those who violate religious
commands should be left to God, and/or that imposing state law
is counterproductive in inculcating religious values. Thus, religious notions of what the state should or should not do with

respect to religious prescriptions is also a question of how one views the relationship between religion and state.

There is no religion in which differences of opinion on this issue do not exist although, one can distinguish major tendencies within Judaism, Islam and Catholicism from Protestantism. The former three religions stress the obligation of the state to "protect" the individual from sinning. (When these religious groups are a minority within a state their attitudes are softened). On the other hand, one can distinguish a major strand within Protestantism which favors separation of religion and state and interprets religion as a system of values which the individual but not the state is obliged to realize — even when Protestants constitute a majority of the society.

But all these caveats to the contrary notwithstanding, religious commitment or faithful adherence to one's religious belief is a good predictor of one's political attitudes. Within the same religion and the same state, those who share the same degree of religious commitment are likely to share the same political positions.

Religious Images

There is a second and far more subtle way in which religion can influence politics. Religion not only projects ideas about what is right and what is wrong, it projects images or conceptions about the nature of the world. These conceptions may penetrate our culture and shape our thinking without regard to whether we are or are not religious believers or religiously observant. Robert Darnton, a recognized authority on French history and culture notes that:

Politics could not take place without the preliminary mental ordering that goes into the common-sense notion of the real world. Common sense itself is a social construction of reality, which varies from culture to culture.[1]

Religious formulations reflect experiences of the past and also shape the way events of the present are experienced. These in turn may become the common sense of a culture. And it is this common sense, these assumption which lay at the root of our ideas about what is right and what is wrong, what will work and what will not work, which policy alternatives are likely to be effective and which are not.

Let us return to the example of abortion. What is our conception of a fetus? Is it a human life, or partially human, or not human at all? Or take the example of eating pig. Is there something essentially immoral or disgusting or unnatural about eating pig? Many Jews and Muslims think there is and they are not necessarily religiously observant. Many Hindus feel the same way about eating the meat of cows. Does this seem far fetched? Then consider the case of bestiality or homosexuality. Now it may be argued that religious prohibitions of homosexuality or bestiality are not religious in origin. It may be argued that they derive from pre-religious notions, perhaps from the need for society to reproduce itself, or from natural instincts. But the same has been said of every religious prohibition — all of them, it is sometimes argued, originate in the functional needs of society. This essay is not concerned with determining whether the abhorrence of bestiality or homosexuality is or is not "natural" or "functional". It is only claimed that the sense of abhorrence or disgust or outrage that some people feel for these acts was transmitted and reinforced by religious norms and serve as illustrations of the cultural penetration of religious conceptions which influence those who are non-religious as well as those who are religious.

Consider another example. How do Jews in Israel view the non-Jew, the *goy* (pl. *goyim*) — the *goy* in Israel, in neighboring states, and in the world in general? Let us not oversimplify the answer. It would be foolish and wrong to argue that all Israeli Jews have the same image of the *goy* (non-Jew, pl. *goyim*), or that all *goyim* are projected as the same by any one Israeli Jew. Nevertheless, a variety of attitude surveys and studies of Israeli culture suggest that most Israelis do have a generalized image of "*goy*" and the image is that of one who is hostile to Jews. Admittedly, this image is grounded in a certain reality. But it is nurtured by what parents, educators, writers, and public officials say about "*goyim*" and about Jewish history. And what they say, what Jews choose to remember and choose to forget in their own history, what they embellish and what they overlook is a function of their preconceptions about *goyim*. Surely the pithy phrase which Rashi, the great medieval commentator cites, "It is well known that Essau hates Jacob," (in which Esau is the paradigm of the *goy* and Jacob the Jew), not only reflects a major tendency within the religious tradition but reinforces that tendency. The notion that *goyim* hate Jews and anti-semitism is a "natural" phenomenon have left their mark on Israeli political culture. Whether this notion is true or false is not the issue here. The point is to demonstrate that religious formulations may become deeply embedded in political culture and thereby shape the way we see the world, the way we interpret facts, and the way we anticipate the consequences of our actions.

It has often been suggested, and there is certainly evidence to support the suggestion, that religion is a great force for conservatism. Voting studies generally find that the more "religious" segment of the population tends to support conservative parties of the right, the less religious or non-religious segment of the population — parties of the left. Religious spokesmen tend to speak out in favor of values of order, of preservation of the status quo in social and economic as well as religious matters. However, there are too many exceptions to this rule to allow for the notion that religion is inevitably conservative. And this should not surprise us.

One view of social change is the capacity of society to respond to a changing environment. But change also takes place in spurts and the notion of change, of something dramatically different, derives from images of a few individuals who successfully convey them as *possible*, in other words as corresponding to reality.

But from where do individuals derive their notion that things can change? And what is the source of their conviction that things ought to change? Did Pharaoh really require a Joseph to tell him that during seven years of plenty he should save grain so that he could feed his population during seven years of famine? Is that idea so brilliant or original? The answer is that it is not brilliant but in ancient Egyptian society it may have been original. In a society where fatalism is the norm and famine perceived as part of the inevitable rhythm of life, one requires an alternative image of reality before one can think of a solution to the problem. Man did not always understand life in a way that enabled him to control it. What leads man to believe that the world can be different than it now is? There is no more important source of such images than religion with its portrait of the "golden age" of the past and/or its vision of the messianic utopian future. Zionism, for example, is inconceivable without Jewish messianic conceptions. These conceptions, one may argue, underwent secularization and owe a great debt to the nationalist formulations of nineteenth century Europe. But this hardly explains why Jews chose to identify their nationalist aspirations in a Jewish context — why all Jews didn't behave as some did, by transferring their national feeling from the Jewish people to that of the peoples among whom they lived.

Much if not all innovation depends upon a belief that things needn't be as they are. But things as they are exert a powerful control over all of us. It is difficult if not impossible for most of us to imagine things very different from the present. How could the grandparents or great grandparents of present day Jews imagine a Jewish state, Jewish sovereignty, Jewish leaders meeting leaders of other nations as equals? How can Israeli Jews imagine themselves living in peace with Arabs or Palestinians while maintaining their ethnic and religious identities? Surely the dream of the Jewish prophets, the notion of "the wolf shall dwell with the lamb and the lion shall lie down with the kid, and nation shall not lift up sword against nation, neither shall

they know war anymore" is for many, whether they call themselves religious or secular, an important vision of the future and,
therefore, a source of how we behave in the present.

Religion may act most often as a conservative force but it has
and continues to act in many societies as a radical force, a force
for change and even for revolution. This is true of the Catholic
Church in many parts of Latin America and Islam in many pre-
dominantly Muslim societies. It is true whether we like or dislike
the particular ideas which the religious revolutionaries convey.
Indeed, if we examine their ideas closely we are likely to find,
even in the case of the former tyrant Khomenie, that we are
sympathetic to at least some of their notions about the need for
and possibility of social reform. It goes without saying that religion in these societies serves to inspire the masses, to organize
them around a particular figure and a particular program but the
argument here is that religion plays a more critical role than that.
Religion imparts the message that a different order of society and
a different type of human is possible. Religion, in its radical role,
breaks convention and consensus. It proposes that there is a
higher order of authority and responsibility than the status-quo
or the existing ruler or present social arrangements or even communal consensus. In other words, even though it bears anti-
democratic tendencies as I will describe in detail, it also carries
the message of a better reality. And this may explain why some
believe that there is no easy answer to the proper role of religion
in politics. Deep commitments to fundamental conceptions of
right and order such as those generated by religion are essential
to the proper functioning of a political system but unless they are
constrained, as we shall see, they can also lead to its disruption.

Religious Structure

The discussion up to this point has argued that religion influences the political system by shaping peoples images and ideas.
It takes for granted that this influence takes place, directly or

indirectly, through the articulation of religious ideas and conceptions. Transmission of this influence takes place initially through sacred texts, through the masters of sacred texts, through the pronouncement of holy men and through priests.

But religion may influence society in other ways. It may do so by the very structure of its organization. Religion presents itself as a system of beliefs and norms which are grounded in the basic nature of the cosmos; religion projects itself as affirming the really real, the ultimate reality. Its strength lies in good part in the fact that it takes itself, even its hierarchical or patriarchal structure or its own mode of interpreting Revelation for granted — as a natural reflection of reality. This assumption by religious leaders and religious masses conveys a very powerful message in traditional societies where religious truths are part of conventional wisdom. But it also has a special power in modcrn societies where all truths have become suspect and where skepticism and doubt are widespread. The very certitude of religion, when it exists, even the pose of certitude may be persuasive for some. Therefore, religion can influence many people not only by what it says but by how it is structured; its hierarchical structure, for example.

It doesn't follow that every person who defines himself as religious necessarily acts in accordance with the demands of his religion. It is all the more true, therefore, that he will not necessarily do what religious leaders insist he do in the political realm. But the influence of religion is more subtle than exhortations to both religious believers as well as to the non-religious to do this or that. A few examples should illustrate this.

The argument which is widely but not universally accepted that Protestantism was the precursor of Democracy is based upon more than Protestant theology, i.e. Protestant ideas about God and the relationship between God and man.[2] It is also based on the importance ascribed to the independent Protestant congregation in which each church established its own rules and the minister was employed by church members serving only at their will. This religious structure or system of governance within the church projected an image of how one ought to be governed and provided the Protestant worshiper with his first experience of self-government that was crucial in shaping images of the proper political system.

Consider the earlier discussion where the different channels in which religion transmits its ideas and conceptions was alluded to. Sacred text and/or masters of text and/or holy men and/or priests all may represent channels of transmission. Different systems of transmission are more important in one religion than in another, in one period than in another, even in one region than another. Although we don't have any firm studies on the subject it seems reasonable to conclude that different emphases ought to have different consequences for one's ideas and images of politics. For example, in religious traditions or among religious groups in which authority is ascribed to masters of sacred text rather than to charismatic holy men it is reasonable to assume that rationalism rather than charisma will have a greater effect on the political behavior of the religious believer and will effect the general political culture as well.

RELIGION AS THE INDEPENDENT OR DEPENDENT VARIABLE

The discussion up till now has focused on the influence of religion on politics. But the relationship is not one-sided. Religion, religious structures, religious beliefs and religious practices, have often been treated by scholars as the consequence of various social and political and more often economic forces in society. These scholars may be labeled "reductionists" for they believe they can explain and therefore "reduce" religion to some other variable. Reductionist explanations of religion characterize Marxist as well as Freudian theories of religion. But almost all scholars tend to interpret whatever data they encounter by utilizing the theories and concepts of their own field with which, of course, they are most familiar and which, of course, makes the most sense to their peers.

The original culprits may have been religious thinkers themselves, particularly in the pre-modern period. Religious leaders as well as simple believers often had a tendency to explain everything in terms of the hand of God. Earthquakes, floods, disease, drought, victory or defeat in war, death or injury in a traffic accident, were and sometimes still are explained by the will of God. We have no argument with that explanation. This is a matter of faith. But the argument becomes reductionist when one assumes that it is an adequate explanation to account for any given event — thereby precluding the laws of nature, or military strategy, or the exercise of care in driving a car or crossing a street.

Just as there are theological reductionists who would explain all events in terms of religious causes, there are academic reductionists who would explain all religious phenomenon, all religious belief or religious behavior in terms of other causes, economic, or psychological, or political. For example, the distinguished sociologist Guy Swanson sought to explain why some societies believed in a High God and others did not. Belief in a High God connotes belief in one God who is superior to all other gods. Swanson, argued that belief in a High God as distinct from belief in many gods who are all roughly equal is a function of the levels of authority within a political system. If the political system is one in which there are three or more levels of authority then belief in a High God prevails. In other words, in a society where the ruler, for example a king or tribal chief, rules the population directly, belief in a High God is unlikely. But in a society with a series of hierarchical levels in which the ruler dominates a second level of rulers who in turn dominate a third level, belief in a High God is likely to prevail because the members of society attribute the characteristics of their form of government to the cosmos.[3] Swanson's argument has been challenged and his theory is no longer as popular as it once was. But it remains a prime example of political reductionism — the effort to explain basic religious belief in terms of political factors.

I am certainly not a reductionist. There are religious impulses, religious ideas and religious demands which have not been and are unlikely to be adequately accounted for by social or political or economic explanations and I do not believe that there is any need to explain them in anything except religious terms. But, by the same token, it is puerile to deny that religious believers and religious thinkers and religious leaders respond to the environment in which they are located — even if they are instrumental in shaping that environment.

Religion responds in a variety of ways and at a variety of levels to its environment. Just as religion influences political culture and the political system in conscious as well as unconscious ways, so the economic, social and political environment can influence religion at both levels. Religious notions about the proper relations between men, about the nature of religious structure, even about God, are influenced by the political environment. Elaine Pagels, an important student of early Christianity has argued, for example, that doctrines that we take to be foundation stones of Christianity are best understood by looking at how they meshed with political conditions in the Roman world and the need of the Church to insure its survival. Indeed, Pagels even argues that Christian doctrines of sexuality are best explained by political conditions of the Roman world.[4] Jeroslav Pelikan has written very important works demonstrating how the Christian image of Jesus changed through the centuries, responding in part to man's changing image of reality.[5] This was even true in the medieval period when religion was so much more important a factor in the lives of Christians. Then, one might have thought, it would be religion influencing society rather than society religion. But both processes took place then as they do today, although the balance in the weight of influence may shift. The point however, is not who influences whom, but how these influences interact. It is often difficult to distinguish cause and effect. Thus, Jacob Katz has shown how Jewish conceptions of the *goy* and of the kind of labor that a *goy* was permitted to perform for a Jew on the Sabbath changed dramatically over the period of a few centuries — not simply because economic or social conditions forced the rabbis to adopt new policies but in a more subtle interrelationship of *halakhah* (Jewish law), theology, economics, politics and culture.[6]

RELIGION, POLITICS AND STATE

Many if not most westerners who think about religion and politics wonder whether it wouldn't be better for both religion as well as for the political system if religion and politics were totally separated? Wouldn't this free religion of the necessity to engage in the compromise if not corruption that is attendant upon involvement in politics? Wouldn't it therefore allow religion and religious leaders to devote themselves to the individual, and to relations between the individual and God which is or ought to be their central concern? And wouldn't it be better for the political system if it didn't have to cope with the religion related demands of religious citizens? After all, these demands are often particularistic, that is they affirm the interests of only one group in society but they are couched in terms that refer to God's will. Most of us don't believe that God's will, at least with respect to questions of public policy, is easily ascertained and in addition, phrasing demands in these terms encourages a sense of fanaticism and zeal destructive of democratic processes. Finally, isn't religion when extended to the political arena incompatible, almost by definition, with democracy? Isn't the absolutism of religion, the authority which the clerics and/or those learned in religious tradition insist upon, in conflict with rule by the majority regardless of who the citizens are, what beliefs they hold, or what religious prescriptions they do or do not observe?

The other side of the coin is that the state is the central agent of the modern political system. It is the major actor, though not the only one, on the international political scene and it is the major arena as well as an objective for those who participate in domestic politics. It is in the context of the state that the unwritten rules of the political game are established and in which, of course, the written laws that govern the society are created and administered. And it is control of the state, in real and symbolic terms, or at least a voice in determining the policies of the state, to which all those engaged in politics set their heart. Can one possibly take any religion seriously if it eschews participation in the political realm?

Among those who believe that religion and politics, for better or worse, are inseparable, there are some who believe that religion should be separated from the state. An attempt to clarify the nature of this dispute is important.

There are many variations of religion-state relationships and strict or total separation is only one of them. In fact, I would argue that strict separation, by definition, is impossible. Separation can only be insured by legislation and the legislation to enforce separation already defines a particular relationship, prohibits religious groups from enjoying a certain authority and prohibits the state from engaging in religious related activity. In other words, strict separation is impossible if only because it can only be legislated and enforced by a state which must, therefore, involve itself in religion. It is a mistake to consider the problem in terms of absolutes.

Some of those who favor separation of religion and state are simply anti-religious. This is true in both Israel and the United States where many strict separationists (among whom Jews are to be found in disproportionate numbers), parade under the banner of "civil liberties" and "private rights" and one has to know them personally to fully appreciate the degree of their anti-religious animus. Their hidden agenda is to destroy religious establishments if not religion itself. But what many others who favor separation of religion and state only want is to insure that the state will make no laws which favor one religion over another religion, or one denomination over another denomination or religion over non-religion. Such demands can and have been made on behalf of religious groups themselves. Certain Protestant denominations are heirs to a political tradition which favors separation of religion and state both as a means of protecting themselves from other Christian denominations but also because their theology justified this demand. But in most cases, certainly in the case of societies where the dominant religion is Judaism, Catholicism or Islam, the demand for separation tends to come either from minority religions who fear discrimination by the dominant religion or from non-religious groups who fear the imposition of religiously based rules which they find coercive and oppressive. For example, marriage laws in Israel require Jews who wish to marry other Jews to undergo a religious ceremony. This is offensive to those who find religious ceremonials objectionable in principle. More commonplace, at least in Israel, is the objection to religious legislation on the basis of inconvenience. For example, objections to the prohibition of opening movie theaters or operating public transportation on the Sabbath is not a matter of religious conscience but does interfere with the style of life which a majority of Israelis wish to pursue.

Among those who favor this kind of separation there is still room for important differences of opinion. There are those who believe that for historical and cultural reasons it is appropriate for the state to remain identified with one religion, at the symbolic level. This is true in England. In Israel, even many of those who favor separation of religion and state continue to favor a special recognition for Judaism, expressed for example, in the symbols of the state which are expressly Jewish and in the very term "Jewish state". Indeed, strict and absolute separation of religion and state in Israel require that it revise its official holidays and days of rest, cease public funding of all religious institutions including religious schools, perhaps even change the name of the country.

There are, therefore, a variety of positions one can adopt with regard to separation of religion and state, although, one can dichotomize those engaged in the struggle, in terms of basic orientation. Therefore, at the risk of repeating some of the points alluded to above, it is useful to summarize the basic arguments for and against separation.

The Case for Separation

The case for separation is based upon a number of considerations. The more important ones include:

First, individual freedom. Religion, we have already suggested, phrases its world-view in absolutist terms. It believes itself possessed of absolute truth. Hence, to the extent that it controls the instrumentalities of the state it is likely to oppress its opponents and deny them basic freedoms. And even when basic freedoms are not denied, religiously based legislation creates inconvenience and discomfort.

Secondly, non-separation is an invitation to group conflict. The separation of religion and state which we find in all western democracies in one form or another (even if it is not as extreme as in the United States), was not achieved solely because people believed in freedom of conscience or freedom of religion. It was achieved after bitter wars and conflict between states and within states. This led many to believe that the only way to maintain public order was to remove the state as a prize for which religious groups might vie. Freedom of religion and freedom from religion introduced an element of stability into the political order.

Finally, in situations where one religion does dominate a society and is sufficiently powerful to insure law and order, the non-separation of religion and state may nevertheless alienate a segment of the public. It will alienate the non-religious who feel that the state discriminates against them. It also alienates other religious groups who will necessarily feel like second class citizens. The problem of Arab Christians in Islamic states is not only the discrimination they may face in the distribution of public money, or in appointments and promotions. There is also the fact that where Islam is part of the very essence of the state Christians are unlikely to feel the same sense of participation in and loyalty to the state that Muslims feel. The alienation of the members of minority religions is compounded by the fact that the members of the majority religion may sense, rightly or wrongly, that since the members of the minority religion are alienated they cannot be trusted; they are inherently disloyal. Such an attitude engenders further alienation.

Non-Jews in Israel face similar problems and they are described in chapter five. The Israeli problem is compounded by the fact that the religious components of Judaism are interrelated with ethnic and national components. They cannot be separated without doing violence to the tradition. However, most Israeli Jews who favor separation of religion and state define religion in a narrow sense and believe they can rid the public sector of religious elements without diminishing the Jewish nature of the state. I believe they are mistaken.

The Case Against Separation

First, the case for separation in the name of religious freedom adopts a particularly Christian-Protestant perspective. It is not coincidental that separation is most extreme in two types of societies — totalitarian ones where the government virtually prohibits religion which it sees as a threat to its control, and in western democratic societies emerging out of a Protestant rather than a Catholic tradition.

There are many Christian groups. They are divided by major doctrinal differences. Nevertheless, one can make certain broad generalizations about Christian doctrine as opposed to Jewish

or Islamic doctrine. The most relevant distinction, for our purposes, is that Christianity focuses upon the individual and his/
her salvation. It is concerned with the fate of the individual's
soul and it provides a means for that soul to be redeemed.
Judaism and Islam exhibit greater concern with the collective
people — the Jewish people (*am Yisrael*) and the community
of Islam (the *umma*). Accordingly, Judaism and Islam maintain
that part of God's revelation to the world includes basic rules
though perhaps not the details as to how society, or in our case
the state ought to be governed. The Catholic Church, because it
assumed societal responsibility in the course of its history also
developed a relatively elaborate conception of the proper
ordering of society.

Protestant groups, in rejecting Catholic doctrine and the practices of the Catholic church, elaborated notions of religion,
already found in Christianity, which emphasized the individual
and ignored the larger collectivity and its political order. This
was not true of all Protestant groups. Indeed, the two main
founders of Protestantism, Luther and Calvin, the latter in particular, placed great importance on the role of the state and the
role of its rulers in imposing proper Christian doctrine. But built
into the very essence of Christianity in contrast to Judaism and
Islam is the notion that the religious community is built upon
individuals who share a belief. Individual Christians come
together to comprise the Christian church. Therefore, one is or
is not a Christian by virtue of whether one does or does not
believe in the basic tenets of Christianity.

Judaism is totally different in this regard. The basic building
block of Judaism is the Jewish people. Being Jewish is a matter
of birth. Jews who do not believe in the basic tenets of Judaism
or who violate Jewish law are sinners, liable to punishment by
the state or by God, but they remain Jews. Judaism is not
entirely particularistic. It is not a tribal religion. It has a univer-
sal message for all mankind. Furthermore, someone born non-
Jewish can convert to Judaism. In other words, Judaism is not a

pure ethno-religion. But since the building block of Judaism is the Jewish people, not the individual who chooses to be Jewish, it follows that Judaism has a great deal to say about the nature of that people and how it ought to be governed. Islam falls somewhere between Judaism and Christianity. In theory it is in many respects closer to Christianity but as Islam worked itself out in its early years of development it assumed a stance which is closer to that of Judaism. This is especially true in Arab societies because Arabs have maintained that there is a special tie between the Arab peoples and Islam.

As a consequence, separation of religion and state is relatively easy to legitimate in Christian, especially Protestant terms. Protestants assume that religion is a private matter since it concerns the individual, how the individual ought to behave, and how the individual achieves salvation. As far as the religiously committed Jew or Muslim is concerned — religion not only imposes obligations upon them as individuals but also upon the collectivity of Jews or Muslims. It obliges the individual believer, therefore, to not only behave in a certain manner in his private life but to engage in politics in order to achieve the social and political objectives which his faith imposes upon the collective Jewish or Islamic people. Separation of religion and state to the Jew or Muslim, especially where the society is composed primarily of Jews or Muslims, is the denial of a basic religious tenet. To say to Jews in a Jewish society or Muslims in an Islamic society that they cannot seek to impose religious conceptions on the public, or alternately that the state cannot impose legislation consistent with the religious demands of Judaism or Islam, is nothing less than a denial of religious freedom.

The second argument against separation of religion and state is more practical than normative but touches so deeply on the essence of the state that it merits mention. No modern state, even the totalitarian state, can achieve its objectives entirely by coercion. The enormous efforts which communist and fascist states invested in persuading their citizens of the legitimacy of the regime is evidence of that fact. States which seek economic development not to mention adequate defense against enemies must mobilize their populations and convince them that it is in their interests to give of themselves on behalf of the state or the society. This effort requires the use of symbols which appeal to the citizens, which resonate for them, and which serve to identify the goals of the state with deeply held beliefs and values. When most of the population is identified with one religion the state will invariably draw upon that religious tradition, especially in a period of crises. Even the Soviet Union, with all of its antagonism to religion, did this during World War II and it would be foolish to believe that every state would not behave in a similar manner under the right conditions. Hence, the argument can be made that separation of religion and the state is contrary to the interests of the state itself — at least where there is one dominant religion. Since I believe that this argument is substantially correct, I want to elaborate upon it because it is not only an unpopular opinion but poses particular problems for a democratic society.

RELIGION AND DEMOCRACY

The relationship between religion and democracy is especially problematic. I turn my attention, first, to the threat which religion poses for democracy. In some cases religion is simply the expression of ethno-national and even class differences that lie at the heart of domestic social conflict. But in addition, religion, despite the prominent role attributed to Protestantism in the birth of the modern idea of democracy, possesses attributes inimicable to democracy as democracy is currently understood in the west.

Elsewhere I have noted that religion socializes its adherents to attitudes and values which challenge, if only by indirection, the attitudinal foundation upon which democracy rests.[7] It seems to me that other things being equal, when religion has no direct stake in public policy, it transmits values which strengthen basic respect for law and authority, a point to which I will return. On the other hand, it does not promote other values essential for a democratic system. I will note three such values.

First, democracy presupposes a large measure of tolerance for the opinions of others, regardless of how sharply one disagrees with these opinions and without regard to the type of person expressing the opinion. Religion, which by definition asserts its possession of the most important truth, tends to generate intolerance toward those who do not share the beliefs and practices which point to that ultimate truth. Religious commitment undermines respect for the opinions of others or the rights of other to express themselves freely when such expression is contrary to basic religious belief. It is folly if not sinful, in accordance with the world view shared by serious religious adherents, to permit the expression of ideas and values which one knows to be wrong, immoral or harmful, especially when such notions are expressed by secularists, whose indifference if not antagonism to basic religious values suggests that they or their intent may be evil. According to a prominent religious Zionist figure, everything published or presented to the public "must be in accordance with moral and educational standards".[8]

Secondly, religion which asserts absolute notions concerning what is right and what is true socializes its adherents to a polarized and dichotomized world. Religion, functioning in the public realm not only sacralizes politics thereby delegitimating compromise, but it imposes a political perspective which tends to demonize one's opponents. The religious believer, other things being equal, is accustomed to the notion that right and wrong, morality and immorality, good and evil, are absolutes and polar opposites, readily distinguishable and pervasive in the political as in all other realms of life. Consequently, religion unintentionally undermines political harmony and intensifies domestic antagonisms.

Finally, religion unlike democracy is less concerned about the process of the political system and more concerned about the outcome or output of the system. Even when religion accepts a democratic political culture in which it is located, it eschews what Robert Bellah calls a liberal constitutional regime which is what democracy has come to mean, rather than a republic. Bellah defines liberal constitutionalism as the notion that "a good society can result from the actions of citizens motivated by self interest alone when those actions are organized through proper mechanisms," and a republic which "has an ethical, educational, even spiritual role..."[9] A religious world view socializes one to the notion that the ideal state is not simply an instrument to serve a variety of interests or needs of the population but a framework to assist one in attaining moral and spiritual elevation. "It is the responsibility of government to protect their own national and religious culture from unacceptable television programs," according to the deputy head of a Saudi owned satellite television network.[10] It is, therefore, insufficient, as far as religious believers are concerned, to be told that the Government has adopted some law in accordance with "due process", i.e. proper procedures or that the majority of the population in addition to a majority of the legislature favor a particular law. Thus, for example, according to a resolution adopted by the Council of Jewish Settlements in Judea, Samaria and Gaza, if Israel should surrender sovereignty over Judea or Samaria it would:

represent a *prima facie* annulment of the State of Israel as a Zionist Jewish state whose purpose is to bring Jews to the sovereign Land of Israel and not, perish the thought, to remove them from the land of Israel and replace them with a foreign sovereignty.[11]

There is no question, therefore, that religion threatens democracy, at least as democracy is increasingly understood in the west. This threat poses a problem for the future because religion is not disappearing.[12]

The solution of choice for secularists is the privatization of religion. Let religion confine itself to matters of the spirit, to the churches, mosques and synagogues, to matters of "individual preferences" and it ceases to pose a problem for the political system. Such a solution is incompatible with a serious commitment to any of the major world religions.[13] It was once thought that at least Buddhism which stresses the virtues of the contemplative monastic life and disdains the material world was compatible with any form of government. But as Donald Smith reminds us, while Buddhism lacks a socio-political doctrine thereby rendering it incapable of leading a social revolution or even pretending, unlike Judaism or Islam, to provide a blueprint for governance, it can overthrow governments and has done so in Burma, Sri Lanka and South Vietnam.[14] In addition, adherents of democracy increasingly stress individual autonomy and this challenges traditional conceptions of education and family. When, as is increasingly the case in stable democracies, such conceptions are incorporated into public policy, religion either clashes with prevailing democratic conceptions or is so emptied of content as to render it totally meaningless.

I suggest that were it possible to privatize religion in a manner that would satisfy secularists, democratic societies would suffer.[15] Democracy, understood as a liberal constitutional system, and this is the logical extension of the meaning of democracy, is self-destructive. Both psychologically as well as legally, individual autonomy undermines the notion of community and collective responsibility. The stress on private rights as an ultimate value, rooted as it is in the notion of the relativity and equality of all values and cultures, leads inevitably to nihilism.[16] Without a sense that there is an absolute truth and an absolute obligation to that truth that transcends the individual and his own needs and appetites, and without the sense that in some way the individual is part of a community that is together obligated to that transcendent truth, I see no possibility for the long term survival of any system of government short of one based totally on coercion. There are differences in the survival capacity of different democratic societies. It matters if the society is one of relative plenty or relative scarcity, if the society is one whose borders are secure or if it faces external threats, if it is a relatively homogenous or heterogenous racial or ethno-religious society, or if the society has a history and tradition of shared purpose or lacks such a history and tradition. But the difference in terms of survival is only one of the time in which it takes to undermine the social order. I am suggesting that western democracies are living on borrowed time; more properly borrowed values of the past which current conceptions of democracy have released from their traditional transcendent moorings and are now in the process of dissolution.

Paul Johnson observes that the focus on the rights of individuals did not erode the foundation of American democracy as long as an unspoken assumption about duties and moral imperatives prevailed.

Congress and the courts could properly concentrate on enforcing rights because the churches, and the ardent men and women who composed them, could safely be left to ensure that all were aware of their duties too, and would perform them.

Once the stress on duties ceases to be sufficiently powerful, or ceases to operate at all among large sections of society, then a rights-based public philosophy tends to break down. There are more human rights, real or imaginary, than there is justice available to satisfy them. When the element of duty is subtracted from the drive for rights, the result is merely a conflict of rights.[17]

Adam Seligman, in his important study on the emergence of the notion of civil society notes that when associations are built around the principle of interest they cannot "mediate or mitigate interest-motivated action in the name of some other or higher ethical unity".[18] Civil society was once capable of doing so but only when

the foundations of moral action were constructed in terms not only of the transcendental principle of Reason but of a transcendent morality as well ... With the loss of these foundations in Reason and revelation, the idea of civil society itself becomes the problem rather than the solution of modern existence.[19]

Religion, I earlier suggested promotes respect for law and authority indirectly as well as directly. I am relying, in this regard, on my intuition and private observations rather than on any published research. But I would be surprised if research were to prove me wrong. It isn't simply that religion, a religious home, a religious school, and religious clerics have a stake, other things being equal, in order and maintenance of authority; it is that religion socializes its adherents to the notion of an orderly purposeful world. In a world of order and purpose the individual is mandated to find his or her proper place. Disturbing the social order is not only improper, in an ultimate sense it is impossible. In addition, religion nurtures the two great anchors of social stability, family and community. It does so in part by sacralizing them but it also does so indirectly. Religion reifies community and family. It imposes them on the imagination of those who share the religious culture as real structures rather than subjective constructs. It has done so, for example, in the state of Israel, where the vast majority of the population defines itself as non-religious but where religious conceptions have permeated the civil culture. This, I believe, is why the Israeli family is an institution of major social importance relative to the family in western democracies where the culture is less permeated by religious conceptions.

It might be argued that nationalism and the symbols, myths and rituals encoded in civil religion might serve as a substitute for traditional religion. But civil religion confronts serious problems. First, in most technologically advanced western democracies, civil religion is unable to resist the increased demands for greater individual autonomy. Indeed, individual autonomy seems to be have become the most sacred value among many western elites. Hence civil religion is viewed with animosity by those elites. Its artificiality and lack of historical roots is easily exposed by an academy anxious to overturn any impediment to individual license. The enormous popularity, in academic circles, of Eric Hobsbawm and Terence Ranger's volume of readings, *The Invention of Tradition*[20], the frequency with which it is quoted when it seems to me that it is quite irrelevant, is testimony to that. The literature which developed in its wake, in England in particular, strikes me as being especially thin but scholarly enthusiasm for this kind of civil religious debunking continues without abate to the applause of rave reviews.[21]

Secondly, in the less technologically advanced democracies, and even among some sectors of the population in the western democracies, civil religion is charged with pretending to substitute itself for traditional religion. The more religiously Orthodox segments of the population, this is especially true in Islamic countries and in Israel, less true in Christian countries, have yet to make their peace with civil religion which legitimates a nationalism which they view as heretical.

Thirdly, even eschewing notions of God and minimizing the symbols borrowed from traditional religion may not be enough for some. Political liberals and radicals, whether they are avowed secularists or religious modernists, increasingly challenge, by direction or indirection, any system that anchors itself in non-contextual morality and any system that affirms transcendent relationships.

It is instructive to compare *The New York Times* coverage of the ceremonies commemorating fifty years to the Normandy invasion with the coverage of that invasion. The ceremony was reported in detail in the June 7, 1994 edition and many of the speeches were summarized. President Clinton's speech was reprinted in full. The virtual absence of references to God was quite striking when one compares the coverage fifty years earlier. The front page of that paper, conveniently reprinted in the 1994 issue, included President Roosevelt's "invasion prayer" which invoked God's help in the "struggle to preserve our Republic, our religion and our civilization, and to set free a suffering humanity." A second front page story was headed, "Country in Prayer" the sub-heading reading "President on Radio Leads in Petition He Framed for Allied Cause". The lead paragraph read:

Led by President Roosevelt, the entire country joined in solemn prayer yesterday for the success of the United Nations armies of liberation.

The story went on to report that the text of the prayer "had been sent out throughout the country and printed in newspapers so that the millions who listened to the broadcast could recite the words with the President as he spoke". Such behavior is inconceivable today, and one cannot help feel that its absence has weakened the capacity of the society to resist threats to its security. On the other hand, as we already noted, religion by its nature is no ally of democracy. This poses a dilemma to which I return chapter four.

CHARACTERISTICS EFFECTING THE INTERRELATIONSHIP OF RELIGION AND POLITICS

The preceding sections stressed that religion and politics influence one another in many indirect and subtle ways and that a primary medium through which this influence takes place is the political culture. But there are more direct types of influences. This section provides a short list of some of the major characteristics of the religious system on the one hand and the political system on the other that effect their interrelationship. As already indicated, we not only want to understand how religious parties and interest groups can influence the society but why religious individuals and groups adopt one policy or another. It is not enough to try and explain this behavior by attributing it to "religious needs" or "religious interests". In some cases these may be based upon material interests. But in many instances it is not clear what factors account for religious groups raising one set of demands rather than another or adopting one set of strategies rather than another. This is the question to which we now turn.

The Important Characteristics of the Religious System

There are three major characteristics of the religious system which we wish to consider: beliefs, values and the religious hierarchy.

Religious belief is among the characteristics of religion which is of significant political importance. For example, does the religion view man as basically rational or irrational? If man is basically rational, then there is a firmer foundation for political alliances with other people and a basis for hoping that political activity will secure the desired results. Religious belief varies from one religion to another, but there are also variations within a given religion. Christianity, for example, is composed of hundreds of denominations and sects. Even within the same religious sub-group, one can identify significant variations in religious belief. Differences between Shia and Sunni Moslems, or between Hasidic and Mitnagdic Jews,[22] and even differences within each of these groups may have political consequences. For example, it is reasonable to assume that religious Jews within the Hasidic tradition are more attracted to charismatic political leaders than Mitnagdic Jews. Finally, religious belief systems are not stable, but rather change in response to pressures from the environment. While in the past changes might have occurred so slowly as to be imperceptible to an entire generation of believers, religion in the post-modern world has been marked by rapid changes in belief. All of this means that whereas religious belief is an important input into any political equation, defining the political consequences of religious belief is far more complex than simply identifying the particular religion in question and then applying a text book definition of its major beliefs.

Let us briefly examine one element of Judaism in its relation to political behavior: the traditional belief in the coming of the Messiah. Belief that the Messiah will come is basic to the Jewish creed, but not all Jews base their political activity on the anticipation of his coming. In other words, the coming of the Messiah is not an operative political belief for all religious Jews. Those who see his coming as imminent will have a different set of political calculations from those who believe in his eventual coming "despite the delay." The first type of believer, anticipating the momentary arrival of the Messiah, is far more liable to be swept into radical and risky political movements because he is already convinced that he will be assisted by supernatural

power, and/or because the natural world is about to be overturned anyway and/or because radical and seemingly irrational
activity constitute a kind of proof, from a religious perspective,
that the individual really believes that the Messiah is about to
come. This is the subject matter of chapter three.

A second characteristic of the religious system that effects
politics is that of religious values. Values, like beliefs, vary from
religion to religion and from one denomination to another within
the same religion. In some religions, or among some sets of
religious believers some values are more important and among
other groups, different values have priority. For example, as a
general rule, political power is a more central value in the
Muslim than in the Judaic religious system. Since its founding,
Islam has stressed the religious significance of its great historical
conquests. Hence, the loss of power by Muslim governments to
the Western colonial powers in the eighteenth and nineteenth
century posed serious theological problems for Islam. Judaism
has long since adjusted to the absence of an independent
Jewish government. In fact, the creation of a Jewish state raised
theological problems for religious Jews. For example, how can
one treat the State of Israel in positive religious terms when its
creators were primarily secular Jews and the vast majority of
religious leaders opposed its creation?

One religious value which traditionally exercised great influence on the political behavior of religious believers was the
importance accorded to activity in "this world" as opposed to the
importance accorded to salvation in "the world to come". Those
religions, and those religious sub-groups which focused on salvation in the world to come were relatively indifferent to political activity. Among such groups, the believer was called upon to
isolate himself from this world. Today, isolation is no longer a
realistic option and there is hardly any religious group which
allows itself to ignore the political arena. Buddhism, the classic
example of an other-worldly religion, has displayed in the last
few generations a dramatic involvement in politics in south-east

Asia, presumably as a result of the threat posed by outside social forces. Even religious groups which pride themselves on their withdrawal from the world are unable to avoid involvement, if only to protect their own boundaries and to insure their continued isolation. For example, the *haredim* (ultra-Orthodox Jews) in Israeli society were primarily concerned with insuring their autonomy and minimizing the influence of the modern secular society on themselves. Paradoxically, in order to achieve the very isolation which they desire, they must involve themselves in Israeli politics — otherwise their children may be drafted into the army, their neighborhoods may be invaded by Sabbath desecrators or the construction of sport stadiums, and they will not benefit from the allocation of any public funds. Nevertheless, distinctions remain between religious groups for whom participation in this-worldly activity is a positive religious value and those for whom it is a necessary evil. Among the former, for example, the political leaders are likely to be the clerical leaders themselves. Among the latter, the political leaders are likely to be spokesmen who act under the guidance of clerical leaders. These differences are of consequence. In the latter case the clerical leaders are likely to remain more insulated from and less sensitive to developments within the general political system and the society at large with all the consequences that flow from such conditions.

A third characteristic of religion with important political implications is its hierarchical organization, especially the relationship between the religious elite and their followers. In some religious groups, the religious leader owes his position to his knowledge of sacred text and his capacity to issue sound judgements based on a superior knowledge and wisdom. Among other groups, the religious leader owes his position to his charismatic qualities: the belief that he possesses special divine gifts. It follows that, other things being equal, the influence of the charismatic leader on the political choices of his followers is likely to outweigh the influence of the rational leader.

We have noted a few of the characteristics of religion which are of importance in influencing the political behavior of their followers or of the society in which the religion plays a role. These characteristics point to what the student of religion and politics might look for. But it is impossible to frame general rules for the inter-relationship of religion and politics, not only because all religions differ from one another but also because within any given religion there are decisive differences from one denomination or sub-group to another. We can state generalizations which tend to hold true for Islam, Judaism, or Christianity, but there are many exceptions to each generalization. For example, until recent years, almost every book on Islam mentioned its inclination to support the status quo as long as the ruler of the society was a Moslem. But the rise of radical Islam, the success of the Ayatollah Khomenie, and the fear that he aroused in the hearts of conservative Muslim rulers, such as those in Saudi Arabia, illustrate the danger of such generalizations.

Some Important Characteristics of the Political System

As was noted earlier, the relationship between religion and politics is dependent not only on the nature of the religion, but also on the nature of the political system with which it interacts. A short list of a few of the major characteristics of political systems which effect that relationship include: the degree of religious pluralism in the society, the degree of religious-state separation, the openness of the society to change, and some socio-economic characteristics that are always politically relevant.

The extent to which religious pluralism exists within a given political system is a significant factor. Is there only one major religion or are there several? Do the different religious groups raise political demands, and if so, does the political culture view such demands as legitimate? For example, Israel appears to be a religiously plural society in the sense that Moslems and Christians enjoy full religious freedom. On the other hand, Israeli society is ruled by Jews and perceives political demands by non-Jewish religious groups as illegitimate. When demands are seen as illegitimate, it is difficult for them to be expressed in the political arena. For example, many religious Jews insist that Israel is obliged, for religious reasons, to annex Judea and Samaria, because according to the Bible, these areas are part of the territory which God promised to the Jewish people. Most Israelis disagree but they do not feel that the demand itself is illegitimate; that religious Jews have no right to voice this demand. In other words, the claims of religious Jews are taken seriously and become a legitimate item on the political agenda. However, if the Israeli Druze, for example, were to claim that in accordance with their religion they were entitled to political independence, these demands would in all likelihood be rejected out of hand. They would not be considered legitimate. In other words, despite religious freedom which non-Jews enjoy in Israel, a legitimacy is accorded to Jewish religious demands at the political level which non-Jewish religions do not enjoy. The nature of the religious demands which are raised and the willingness of the society to consider them is a consequence of the extent to which religious pluralism is tolerated by the political system. If religious demands are not considered legitimate it makes it much more difficult and much less likely that they will be raised. And if they are raised, since they are not legitimate, they can only be pressed outside the legitimate political arena — that is through demonstrations and possibly violence.

Another important dimension of the political system is the degree of and assumptions about religious-state separation. There are great variations in political systems and political cultures. In some, such as the United States or the former Soviet Union, separation of religion and state is more of a basic principle than in others. For example, efforts on the part of religious groups in the United States to influence public policy are generally accompanied by apologies and/or by justifications phrased in secular terminology. When religious groups in the United States attempt to restrict abortions they present their arguments in terms of "the right to life" rather than as a religious commandment. When religious schools in the United States request government assistance they do not do so on the basis of the fact that children from religious homes are entitled to a religious education at the expense of the state. Instead, religious schools will request assistance for specific programs such as library books, transportation of the children to and from school, or lunch programs, which, they argue, the state ought to provide for all children because these services have nothing to do with religion. In other societies, such as Israel, non-separation is so taken for granted that even many Israelis who think of themselves as totally secular accept the idea that the government should pay rabbi's salaries, allow the Knesset to decide how the chief rabbis are to be elected, and support religious schools on the same basis that it supports non-religious schools.

A third important dimension of the political system is the extent to which it is open to demands for political change. Such openness may be related to the extent to which the system is authoritarian or democratic, but alternatively, it is sometimes related to the extent to which the political system is autonomous; in which the political leadership can institute and implement policy.

The relative autonomy of the political system has another consequence for religion. It was not uncommon for religion and religious customs to flourish under colonial governments: this was often the only field in which the colonial ruler permitted total autonomy to the local subjects. Religion, in such instances, became a symbol of the desire for national independence. To this day, ethnic or national tensions and sometimes even economic tensions may assume the guise of religious competition. Religion, in other words, is a very useful symbol around which different types of groups may organize in order to press demands that are not necessarily of a religious nature. The role of the Roman Catholic church in Poland under Communist rule is only one such example.

The final dimension of the political system, the economic and social structure, is not strictly speaking political, but it is so interrelated with politics that it cannot go unmentioned. Is the economy basically rural or urban? Agricultural or industrial? Developed or backward? To what extent is there an equal division of financial resources in the society? These factors, and others related to them, are influential in determining the role of religion in the political system. Generally, religion plays a more important role in those societies which are rural, agricultural and backward. Another factor which undoubtedly plays a major role is the degree to which there is free and rapid social mobility in the society. Where some groups can be seen to be highly mobile, other, relatively deprived groups often express their frustrations in the political arena in religious language.

These are the basic questions and issues which define the field of religion and politics. In the next four chapters I hope to illuminate some of them by describing how they are played out in Israel.

ENDNOTES

1. Robert Darnton, *The Great Cat Massacre and Other Episodes in French Cultural History* (New York: Vintage Books, 1985), p. 23.
2. The question of the relationship between religion and democracy in general, Christianity and democracy in particular, and Protestantism and democracy more specifically has been of intermittent interest to students of society but with some notable exceptions (e.g. S. N. Eisenstadt, "Cultural Traditions and Political Dynamics," *British Journal of Sociology*," 32 ((1981)), pp. 155–181) scholars have looked at the question from the context of a particular religious tradition or a particular area. The question has been approached from a variety of theoretical and empirical perspectives. Despite the compelling nature of the theoretical arguments that have been advanced for the positive relationship between Protestantism and development of a political culture conducive to democracy, the empirical evidence is inconclusive. The most recent literature also suggests that the question does not admit of any comprehensive answer. See, for example, James C. Cavendish, "Christian Base Communities and the Building of Democracy: Brazil and Chile," *Sociology of Religion*, 55 (Summer, 1994), pp. 179–195.

3. Guy Swanson, *The Birth of the Gods: The Origin of Primitive Beliefs* (Ann Arbor: University of Michigan Press, 1960).

4. Elaine Pagels, *Adam, Eve and the Serpent* (New York: Random House, 1988).

5. Jaroslav Pelikan, *Jesus Through the Centuries: His Place in the History of Culture* (New Haven: Yale University Press, 1985).

6. Jacob Katz, *The "Shabes Goy": A Study in Halakhic Flexibility* (Philadelphia: Jewish Publication Society, 1989).

7. "Religion and Democracy in Israel," in Ehud Sprinzak and Larry Diamond (eds.) *Israeli Democracy Under Stress: Cultural and Institutional Perspectives* (Boulder: Lynne Rienner, 1993), pp. 273–292 and also "Attitudes Toward Democracy Among Israeli Religious Leaders," Edy Kaufman and Shukri Abed (eds.), *Democracy, Peace and the Israeli Palestinian Conflict* (Boulder: Lynne Rienner, 1993), pp. 135–161.

8. The speech by Rabbi Haim Druckman was reprinted in *Nekudah*, March 2, 1983 and is described in Charles S. Liebman, "Jewish Ultra-Nationalism in Israel: Converging Strands," in William Frankel (ed.), *Survey of Jewish Affairs, 1985* (London: Associated University Presses, 1985), pp. 28–50.

9. Robert Bellah, "Religion and the Legitimation of the American Republic," in Robert Bellah and Phillip Hammond, *Varieties of Civil Religion* (New York: Harper and Row, 1980), p. 9. The point and its application to Israeli society is discussed more fully in Charles S. Liebman and Eliezer Don-Yehiya, "The Dilemma of Reconciling Traditional Culture and Polit-ical Needs: Civil Religion In Israel," *Comparative Politics* (October, 1983), pp. 53–66.

10. *Newsweek* March 2, 1994, p. 46.

11. The statement was issued November 4, 1985, reprinted in *Davar*, November 22, 1985 and translated into English in International Center for peace in the Middle East, *Israel Press Briefs*, 40 (December, 1985), p. 17. There are many similar statements.

12. A most instructive volume on this topic is Steve Bruce (ed.), *Religion and Modernization: Sociologists and Historians Debate the Secularization Thesis* (Oxford: Oxford University Press, 1992).

13. On the problem of transforming religion into a matter of individual preference see Peter Berger, *A Far Glory: The Quest for Faith in an Age of Credulity* (New York: The Free Press, 1992).

14. Donald Eugene Smith, "Limits of Religious Resurgence," Emile Sahliyeh (ed.), *Religious Resurgence and Politics in the Contemporary World* (Albany: SUNY Press, 1990), p. 38.

15. The notion that the social functions which religion provides are an important if not a necessary component to the functioning of democracy is hardly new. Its most recent articulation is Stephen L. Carter, *The Culture of Disbelief: How American Law and Politics Trivialize Religious Devotion* (New York: Basic Books, 1993).

16. That notion is stated most forcefully and I think convincingly in Ernest Gellner, *Postmodernism, Reason and Religion* (New York and London: Routledge, 1992). See also James Hunter, *Before the Shooting Begins* (New York: The Free Press,

1994), p. 31. It is echoed in any number of recent works such as Jeane Bethke Ellshtain, *Democracy on Trial* (New York: Basic Books, 1994) and Christopher Lasch, *The Revolt of the Elites and the Betrayal of Democracy* (New York: W.W. Norton, 1995) which led a reviewer to suggest that:

The ruling American culture of liberal individualism treats communal attachments and civic engagement as optional extras on a fixed menu of individual choice and market exchange ... Now that the Soviet collapse has deprived the American Government of the legitimacy it borrowed from the cold war, it is difficult not to foresee a further weakening of the civic culture in the United States. John Gray, "Does Democracy Have a Future?," *The New York Times Book Review* (January 22, 1995), p. 25.

17. Paul Johnson, "God and the Americans," *Commentary* vol. 99 (January, 1995), p. 41.
18. Adam Seligman, *The Idea of Civil Society* (New York: The Free Press, 1992), pp. 197–198.
19. *Ibid.*, p. 198.
20. Eric Hobsbawm and Terence Ranger (eds.), *The Invention of Tradition* (Cambridge: Cambridge University Press, 1983).
21. An explanation for the enthusiasm of so many academics is found in Anthony Smith, "The Nation: Invented, Imagined, Reconstructed?" *Millennium: Journal of International Studies*, 20, no. 3 (1991), pp. 353–368.
22. Hasidic Jews are divided into a variety of groups distinguished primarily by their devotion to their charismatic leaders whom they call their *rebbe*. The best known of the hassidic groups is Habad, or Lubavitcher hasidim. Mitnagdim or *Litvish* (Lithuanian) Jews, are Orthodox Jews whose central leaders are the great Talmudic sages most of whom are heads of academies for Talmudic study. Their source of authority resides primarily in their knowledge of sacred text.

TWO

The Struggle Among Religious Zionists over the Issue of a Religious State

Asher Cohen and Charles S. Liebman

Political parties and interest groups with religious objectives are likely to have an impact on public policy. That much is obvious. Less obvious is that political participation and the effort to achieve political goals by religious parties and interest groups will influence their religious conceptualizations. This chapter deals with this point and with the question of religious innovation. Religious innovation, as we shall see, is also influenced by political participation.

Institutions, like living organisms, do not survive unless they respond to their environments. Response does not necessarily mean affirmation. There are three models for the manner in which religious groups and movements respond. They may affirm their social and cultural environment, they may reject the environment and withdraw from it or they may resist the environment and seek to transform it. In practice, intermediate forms are also possible.

Religions in the Abramic tradition have generally accommodated, gradually and unself-consciously to social and cultural changes in their environment. This accommodation is reflected in changes or new interpretations, sometimes barely perceptible, in religious symbols, norms and myths. But in periods of rapid social and cultural change religions may seek to innovate in a more self-conscious manner. The question of religious innovation is, in one sense, a specific case of the more general process of institutional innovation. But it is a special case because religion is limited in its ability to legitimate innovation. Religious groups and movements must legitimate their innovations in terms of processes endemic to the religious system. This chapter deals with some strategies of religious innovation. These strategies, as we shall see, don't always work. Both innovation and the impact of political participation on religious conceptions are examined through a case study of a problem that beset the religious-Zionist movement in the early years of Israeli statehood. Hence, it is necessary to understand something of the nature of religious-Zionism in order to understand the story of this chapter.

Religious-Zionism is best comprehended as an ideological family and the best way to explain the ideology of religious-Zionism is to separately examine each of the terms which constitute its name.[1] First of all, religious-Zionists share a commitment to the Jewish religion and to observance of Jewish law — to what is called Orthodox Judaism. But the Orthodoxy to which religious-Zionists adhere became increasingly distinctive by the beginning of this century. That which distinguishes religious-Zionists from Orthodox Jews who are not Zionists, at least until most recently, is the former's accommodating, indeed positive attitude toward modernity.[2] They favored, at least until recently, secular education and the package of values we generally associate with modernity and secular education — among them the values of democracy and individual liberty.

In the first two decades of the present century the nascent Zionist movement became more explicitly secular in its orientation. As a result many religious Jews withdrew their support from the Zionist enterprise. Those who remained, i.e. those religious-Zionists who didn't resign their membership or withdraw their support from the Zionist movement were those religious Jews who either found Jewish secularism less offensive and/or were so imbued with Zionist belief and so committed to the unity of the Jewish people that they were prepared to overlook the slights to religion that increasingly characterized Zionist activity and Zionist ideology.[3] In other words, those religious Jews who remained both Zionists and Orthodox Jews are distinguishable from other Orthodox Jews in their tolerance if not sympathy for new modes of thinking and behaving.

So much for the term "religious". Before 1948 the term Zionism, for religious-Zionists, meant the effort to establish a Jewish state, in cooperation with all other Zionists and without regard to how religious or irreligious or anti-religious the others were. Since 1948 and the establishment of Israel, Zionism has meant an appreciation of the central role of the Jewish state in Jewish life. There is a more subtle meaning to the term Zionist which has to do with the nature of the Jewish people but which needn't concern us in this chapter.

To return to matters of definition, religious-Zionism is a hyphenated word. Its ideology is more than the total of religion plus Zionism. Religious-Zionism affirms the belief that the Zionist enterprise in general, the establishment of the state of Israel in particular, and the development of the state since 1948 reflects in some special way the will of God. It signals, as we shall describe in the next chapter, the beginning of the promised redemption for the Jewish people and ultimately the whole world. The state of Israel, in other words, has special religious significance. It is therefore incumbent on Jews, those who live in Israel in particular, to conduct their lives in accordance with this special religious significance that accrues to its very existence. And it is no less incumbent on the political leaders of the state to formulate public policies in the same manner.

Religious-Zionist history goes back to the middle of the nineteenth century. Indeed, the forerunners of modern Zionism might be described, in retrospect, as religious-Zionists.[4] Many of the nominal leaders, some of the real leaders and many if not most of the masses of Jews active in the earliest Zionist movements in Russia beginning in 1881 were, if not religious-Zionists at least both religious and Zionists.[5] The vast majority of the first modern Jewish settlers in Palestine, i.e. those whom came in the 1880's and 1890's to establish an economically self-sufficient Jewish society were certainly Orthodox Jews by today's standards of religious observance. But the organizational history of religious-Zionism begins with the founding of Mizrachi, a party within the World Zionist Organization, in 1902.[6]

Despite the conviction of the party's first leader, Rabbi Isaac Jacob Reines, about the need to find an immediate solution to the material needs of the Jewish people (hence his willingness to consider havens outside the Land of Israel), and the desirability of cooperating with all Zionists regardless of their religious orientations,[7] Mizrachi's declared purpose remained the establishment of a Torah state. Religious-Zionists disagreed over economic policy, over relations with the Arabs, over relationships with the *haredim*, i.e. the ultra Orthodox Jews who opposed Zionism, and over relationships with the secular Zionists who opposed religion but they all affirmed the slogan, first coined by Mizrachi, "the Land of Israel, for the People of Israel, in accordance with the Torah of Israel". Admittedly the nature of such a state remained vague but the vision of *medinat HaTorah*, a Torah state, i.e. a state conducted in accordance with the mandates of Jewish law, was shared by all religious-Zionists.

Religious-Zionists were always a minority within the Zionist movement and among the Israeli electorate. A generous estimate of the percentage of religious-Zionists in 1948, at the time of the establishment of Israel, would still give them less than 15 percent of the Jewish population. In the period preceding the establishment of the state, the highest percent of the votes that religious-Zionist parties obtained was in 1944 when they won 13 percent although then as now, not all religious-Zionists voted for religious-Zionists parties. At the beginning of the period on which this chapter focuses, the period from 1947 to 1955, there were two religious-Zionist parties and two *haredi*, i.e. non-Zionist ultra-Orthodox religious parties. All four parties ran on one list in the first Knesset elections held in 1949. They won

16 seats or roughly 13 percent of the 120 member Knesset. In the second Knesset elections the two religious-Zionist parties, running independently, won ten seats and less than ten percent of the vote. The *haredi* parties won five seats. In the third Knesset election in 1955 the two religious-Zionist parties ran on one list, and won eleven seats whereas the two haredi parties won six seats.

Religious-Zionism at that time was closely tied, even more so than today, with the chief rabbinate of Israel and with a large rabbinical establishment. Even then *haredim* had a strong influence over the rabbinical establishment, but it is stronger today than it was forty to fifty years ago for reasons that needn't concern us here.[8]

The declaration by the United Kingdom that it was withdrawing from Palestine focused U.N. attention on that area and aroused the anticipation of the Jews for an independent state. On November 29th 1947 the United Nations voted to partition Palestine. The consequences would be the establishment of a Jewish state in part of the territory. It is in this period that religious-Zionists appreciated the immediate need to operationalize their notion of a Torah state. After all, there was, up till then, no outline, not to mention detail about what a state governed in accordance with Torah meant. The absence of such considerations in the past, now evoked self criticism and guilt feelings within the ranks of religious-Zionism. Under the new conditions of statehood, important religious-Zionist figures felt that the movement was obliged to reexamine its direction. One of its major ideologues, Shlomo Zalman Shragai, for example, wrote:

Let us imagine for a moment that we succeeded [electorally] and a majority of the Knesset says: We are ready to run the state according to the Torah ... Is religious Judaism ready to say: here is the program!? ... Certainly not! ... But it is to be found within the Torah. And it requires study. It requires effort and investment.[9]

The major players, in the first instance, were important rabbinical figures. Chief among them, really the central rabbinical figure, was Israel's first Ashkenazi chief rabbi, Isaac Herzog, former chief rabbi of Ireland, a renowned rabbinical scholar, at home in the world of secular knowledge and socialized to contemporary western values as well.

In retrospect one might wonder at this effort. Did religious-Zionists who constituted a small minority of the Jewish population really believe they could succeed in imposing their vision of a Torah state, through democratic procedures, and no other means were ever contemplated, on a secular majority which included many political leaders and many cultural leaders who were antagonistic to the religious establishment and indeed to religion in general? Part of the answer to this question is tied to the religious excitement which the anticipation and creation of a Jewish state aroused in those years.

The period surrounding the creation of a Jewish state, was perceived by religious-Zionists as a momentous period in which all the evidence seemed to demonstrate God's direct intervention in events. The expectation that a Jewish state would be conducted in accordance with the Law of Moses, i.e. of God, must have seemed less far fetched then, more capable of realization.

From the very outset, two conflicting views emerged about the nature of a Torah state. Whereas one view sought to minimize the changes which the new condition of statehood imposed, the second view, in a play on words, has been labeled *kiddush he'hadash*, the sanctification of the new. We prefer to use the term "innovative Orthodoxy". The characteristic demands of those who favored this position, and there were nuanced differences among them were:

First, reducing reliance upon past *halakhic* decisions and expanding the authority of contemporary religious leaders. The *halakhic* system, i.e. the system of Jewish law, tends to be very conservative. *Halakhic* decisors are always uncomfortable when they are accused of innovating, an accusation that they are by definition bound to reject. *Halakha* is a system of religious law which is perceived by its advocates as basically an interpretation of Divine will as recorded in the Torah and the Talmud, i.e. the written and the oral law. Furthermore, it is a system of interpretation rather than legislation. Rabbinic authorities accept the principle that the earlier the period in which a decision was reached the greater is its authority (the earlier the age of the authority the closer it is in time to the Sinai epiphany and the more reliable the information orally transmitted from Sinai). Hence, rabbinic authorities will never rule in opposition to earlier authorities. They innovate, in practice, by choosing from among conflicting opinions and/or by defining the problem they are asked to resolve to coincide with one paradigm rather than another. But innovation in this manner is limited. Furthermore, its very limitation establishes a climate of opinion among the legal authorities which further emphasizes the value of continuity over the value of change.

The innovative view sought to legitimate basic revisions in the process of *halakhic* decision making by exploiting the religious-Zionist belief that the creation of a Jewish state signaled a new stage in the process of Redemption. If Jews have entered a new stage of human history, past traditions and past rabbinic leaders are less authoritative. The new era requires and legitimates a new religious leadership which can and must be more innovative.[10]

Related to this first point was the second characteristic notion of those who favored the innovative position. They argued that contemporary rabbinic authorities could innovate while retaining their fidelity to the tradition because the tradition should be viewed as a system of general rules that provide guidance for contemporary rabbinic authorities rather than a system of specific law which constrains contemporary authorities.[11]

Thirdly, the proponents of this view felt that under certain circumstances, given the new conditions under which the Jewish people now lived, that which was heretofore deemed deviation, would be legitimate. A good example of this is the problem which Yeshayahu Leibowitz raised of police activity on the Sabbath. It is a hard and fast rule of Jewish law that one can violate the Sabbath to save a life. But one cannot violate the Sabbath to save one's property. How, therefore, can one conduct a police force in accordance with Jewish law? The police can be out on patrol, ostensibly violating the Sabbath, because of a possible threat to life. But what if they witness a robbery in progress in which human life is not threatened? There is no basis in Jewish law allowing them to arrest the thief. And if the police force does not conduct itself in accordance with religious law may a religiously observant Jew serve as a policeman when such service will involve him in Sabbath violations? Are religious-Zionists to preclude the devout Jew from performing what is admittedly a legitimate state function? To those who favored the innovative approach of sanctifying the new, the choice seemed clear.

There was a final and most extreme point to the innovative conception, the notion of "the authority of the public" and we will return to this in our concluding discussion. It didn't really arise until other strategies had failed.

The consequences of adopting the innovative perspective was probably clear to its adherents even if they never articulated them. It meant a break with the Orthodox tradition in which they had been raised and which they were presumably committed to preserve. This suggests to us that those who espoused this program, certainly in its more radical version, were far more ambivalent if not rebellious toward the religious tradition than anyone who now claims to be a religious-Zionist is wont to believe. Secondly, adopting such a program would have meant a total break with the *haredi* world, something many innovators might have welcomed. But less welcome would have been a third consequence, a split in the religious-Zionist movement.

How are we to understand the radical nature of the innovative wing within religious-Zionism? First of all, we must recall that religious-Zionism was always radical and innovative when compared to the *haredi* world. There was an element of religious radicalism that religious-Zionists themselves, consciously or unconsciously acknowledged as inherent in the movement. In addition, as we indicated above, religious-Zionists, the more radical wing in particular, sensed that the creation of the state ushered in a new era in human history that justified innovation in the tradition. Added to that was the fact that the Holocaust also left its mark both materially and psychologically. The Holocaust was incomprehensible to religious-Zionists in theological categories. They rejected out of hand the notion that the Holocaust was a punishment for the sins of the Jews which in the *haredi* version was primarily the sin of Zionism. But, though theologically incomprehensible, perhaps because it was theologically incomprehensible, religious-Zionists still sensed the Holocaust as a dramatic turning point in Jewish history signalling something new. And since there was an imprecision about what that something new really meant it allowed religious Jews to interpret its meaning in a manner which suited their own proclivities.

We can better understand the radicalism of innovative Orthodoxy if we also understand who their referents were, and were not. The Holocaust destroyed the *haredi* world centers. *Haredi* reorganization in both Israel and the diaspora lay in the future. In the late 1940's and early 1950's, *haredim* did not constitute as significant an influence in Jewish or even religious life as they would in the coming decades. Not only had their centers vanished but the insensitivity of *haredi* leaders to the consequences of Hitler's rise to power and their continued opposition to Zionism, although emigration to Palestine, in retrospect, was the safest haven for eastern European Jewry, reduced their status as significant references for religious-Zionists. Finally, we must recall that in those days, this may be the most difficult of all to recall, secular Zionism carried enormous status ethically and morally for religious-Zionists. In fact, religious-Zionists in general, and its most radical wing, the religious kibbutz movement in particular, sought to emulate the standards that were set by secular Zionism, socialist-Zionism in particular.[12] Innovative

Orthodoxy looked over its shoulder to its left to find its significant reference group; there was no reference group to its right.

Kiddush he'hadash, sanctifying the new, reforming the tradition was one view of the parameters which ought to guide the
operationalizing of the Torah state. The second view is the
more obvious one and can be treated more summarily. It was
the traditional view of "fidelity to the old". According to this
view, it is the newborn Jewish state that must adjust itself to the
religious tradition — to *halakha.* The requirements of a modern
state and the value of democracy and individual liberties are
obligatory only in so far as they don't contradict the religious
tradition. The process by which the tradition itself is to be interpreted would remain the same although there was an acknowl-
edgement that rabbinic authorities might have to adopt a bold
course in confronting issues that had never arisen in the past.
To cite one dramatic example, the question arose whether non-
Jews ought to enjoy the same religious and even civil rights
that Jews enjoy in a Jewish state. The issue is not as simple as
one might think. When medieval commentators discussed the
topic of religious liberty and civil rights of non-Jews, they
phrased their formulations in circumstances under which Jews
lacked any political power and limited religious rights. When
they speculated on the hypothetical condition of Jewish power,
in the Holy Land no less, they were inclined to hold that the
liberties of non-Jews ought to be constrained. Apologists are
correct that when the medieval commentators discussed Jewish
power over non-Jews in the Holy Land they were describing a
utopian-messianic condition. But the fact is that they were also
formulating a religious ideal. All religious-Zionists acknowledged that in the new state, even in a new Torah state, no
effort should be made to realize that ideal. But how was this to
be justified? The most significant figure in this discussion, Rabbi
Herzog, did so by offering a variety of arguments centering
around the same notion — the United Nations, or the nations of
the world were partners, perhaps even senior partners in the

creation of the state. Hence, that which would be incumbent on Jews acting alone, was not incumbent upon them by virtue of their partnership. For example, he maintained that the commandments obliging us to discriminate against non-Jews:

> ... were only decreed under circumstances when the Jewish people conquer the Land and assume sovereignty on their own, without regard to the Gentiles... In the absence of these circumstances, and given the conditions under which the state is given [to us, by the United Nations], these commandments do not hold.[13]

He also suggested that if full freedoms were denied non-Jews, the United Nations would never agree to the establishment of the Jewish state so the whole question would become mute.

Herzog dared not, we would like to believe he wanted to but he dared not, deny the ideal which a number of the medieval commentators had established. To some extent, we are paying the price today, for the reluctance to confront this aspect of the tradition head on.

But let us not be too quick to judge. The office of the chief rabbinate, and chief rabbi Herzog in particular, had to confront the dilemma of a Torah state in its keenest form. Herzog and his colleagues were caught between a variety of tensions. There was a personal tension — the values of modernity which Herzog in particular espoused and the values of the religious tradition. Secondly there was an institutional tension between what was then a sincere feeling on the part of the chief rabbis that they ought to represent, at least in some respects, all the Jews of Israel, not only a religious constituency, and their obligation to *halakha*, regardless of how unpopular its tenets might be. And finally there was the political tension between the rabbis' obligations and responsibility to the nation's political leaders whom they also admired, an obligation and admiration which the chief rabbis in those days sincerely felt, and their responsibility to the rabbinical world, a rabbinical world in which *haredi* influence may have diminished but had not disappeared. We must recall that a major difference between the innovative Orthodox and those who would preserve the old is that few rabbis and only two of any stature (one of whom switched sides in the middle of the controversy anyway), were numbered among the innovators. The camp of the traditionalists was led by rabbis who were necessarily responsive to the *haredi* world, indeed to a *haredi* world whose spiritual and material center no longer existed but whose passing they mourned. This is particularly true of Rabbi Herzog. We know from his own writing that precisely because of the particularly destructive effect of the Holocaust on the *haredi* world, he felt special obligations toward it.[14]

Herzog's letters and notes testify that he strove mightily to find a way to square the demands of Jewish law with the requirements of a modern state and modern conceptions of democracy and justice. But he alludes to three impediments which suggest, at least in retrospect, the futility of his efforts. Herzog notes that whereas he was prepared to press Jewish law "to the farthest most radical boundaries," most of his colleagues objected to any change.[15] Secondly, it was they who pointed out that regardless of how permissive or accommodating of modernity he would be, and regardless of how far he pushed the limits of Jewish law to accommodate the needs of a modern democratic state and its political leaders, "we will never satisfy their thirst for changes".[16] Finally, Herzog himself wondered if all the recommendations for change would not render Jewish law into a secular subject foreign to those who had mastered traditional sources of Jewish law.[17]

The second major group of players who also abandoned the effort to operationalize the provisions of a Torah state were the political leaders of religious-Zionism. Two reasons suggest themselves. First of all, as already suggested, once the vision of a Torah state was translated into specific provisions it would either emphasis the requirements of a contemporary democratic society which required a radical reinterpretation of *halakha* and thereby lead to the withdrawal of the more traditional elements within religious-Zionism; or it would subordinate the requirement of a modern democratic state to the classical interpretation of Jewish law and thereby lead to the withdrawal of the smaller but nonetheless prestigious innovative elements. This more innovative element was led by the religious kibbutz movement which was the demonstration piece of religious-Zionism. It then served as proof that religious-Zionism also deserved a place in the pantheon of pioneer heroes who established the state. In either case the religious-Zionist movement would be weakened.

The second reason political leaders became increasingly skeptical about efforts to operationalize the notion of a Torah state had to do with political priorities. These leaders sat in the Knesset as representatives of religious voters. They were engaged, in the early years of statehood, in a life and death struggle with anti-religious and non-religious elements over specific Knesset legislation. It was not clear, in those days, that the religious school system would be autonomous, that religious courts would be permitted to exercise independent authority, that Jews who refused to violate the Sabbath would not be discriminated against in matters of employment, that new immigrants would not be coerced into violating Jewish law as was done to Yemenites in the immigrant camps. The religious atmosphere in Israel was entirely different in those years than it is today. The political representatives of the religious camp, and not only the religious-Zionist camp, had their hands full in mobilizing their constituents in defense of interests that they viewed as basic. They had neither the energy nor did they see the point in engaging in an acrimonious debate over a purely hypothetical question concerning the nature of a Torah state which would not only split their own party but sever them from allies among the non-Orthodox representatives in the Knesset. Ben-Gurion often declared, perhaps in partial response to the publicity attendant on the effort to formulate the provisions of a Torah state, that Israel was to be a state based upon law and not upon *halakha*. This declaration won the assent of all the non-religious parties and the overwhelming majority of Israelis. As far as the political leaders of religious-Zionism were concerned, the real struggle in the words of its preeminent political leader Moshe Shapiro, was "over the image and the character of the state of Israel from a religious perspective".[18] Therefore, Shapiro declared:

I do not believe in the possibility of adapting the demands of the Torah to all that a modern state requires. It's easy to talk about it, but very hard to realize it in reality.[19]

By the beginning of the 1950's, therefore, it seemed clear, in retrospect, that the vision of a Torah state was not to be operationalized. But that which is clear in retrospect was not clear at the time, at least not to all the parties concerned. It was not clear to the masses of religious-Zionists among whom the religious excitement of a Jewish state had not yet diminished and who, raised on the vision (slogan) of "The Land of Israel, for the People of Israel, In Accordance with the Torah of Israel" demanded continued efforts to operationalize the vision. This was a demand which the more radical elements in the religious-Zionist camp were especially anxious to nurture. Their cry was enhanced by the fact that neither the chief rabbinate or the political leaders, with the exception of Shapiro, dared express the theoretical hopelessness or the political futility of such an effort. Indeed, the chief rabbinate could do little more than listen in silence when they were castigated in religious-Zionist circles for their feeble efforts to provide detailed provisions for a Torah state. In theory there had to be a solution to the problem, otherwise the vision itself would be rendered meaningless. Since nothing had been done about it, the rabbinate, the chief rabbinate in particular, stood accused of cowardice, lack of initiative, or lack of commitment.[20] The solution which some now favored, was to transfer *halakhic* authority from the chief rabbinate to some other source.

This was an inherently dangerous step for religious-Zionists who, in many respects needed the chief rabbinate no less and perhaps more than the chief rabbinate needed them. The chief rabbinate was religious-Zionism's answer to the *haredi* charge that religious-Zionism lacked religious legitimacy. Whereas *haredim* submitted themselves to the authority of great Talmudic scholars, organized in a body known as the Council of Torah Sages which ostensibly dictated the policies of the *haredi* parties, the religious-Zionists submitted to no recognized *halakhic* authority. The religious-Zionists, however, pointed to the office of the chief rabbinate as their authority. So any effort, then as now, that undermined the authority of the chief rabbinate, particularly its authority over the religious-Zionist parties, was fraught with danger.[21]

The least radical proposal, one that was easily approved, was the creation of a rabbinic body within the largest religious-Zionist party. It was called *Hever HaRabbanim shel Hapoel Hamizrachi*. The rabbis who formed this group hoped to encourage greater effort toward explicating the meaning of a Torah state. Toward that end they sponsored the publication of a new journal *HaTorah V'Hamedina* (Religion and State). The chief rabbinate was unhappy with the creation of a politically inspired rabbinical body. Herzog himself only permitted the new publication to reproduce two or three of his previously published articles and he offered no new contribution to the journal. But those who hoped that the new body would be more innovative in its *halakhic* perspective were to be soundly disappointed. In the very first issue of the new journal, the new group made it clear that they would not challenge the chief rabbinate's authority.

The second solution is the most widely known, probably because it was initiated by one of the most prominent religious-Zionist leaders, something of an iconoclast in religious matters, the Minister of Religion, Rabbi Yehuda Leib Maimon. Maimon proposed the creation of a Sanhedrin, i.e. the reestablishment of the great Court of judges-legislators that sat during the later part of the second Temple period, and according to Jewish tradition not only adjudicated matters but, in fact, served as a legislative body with power to innovate religious law. Such a body, the innovators argued, was justified, given the new period in which we are living. It was hoped that this body, possessed of powers that no other body of religious authorities had possessed since the destruction of the Temple, would legislate in daring and dramatic directions.

This is not the place to attempt to demonstrate why, even had the Sanhedrin been created, it is unlikely to have acted as the innovators had hoped. The unreasonable expectation that it might do so can only be attributed, once again, to the *stirrings*, to use that felicitous Protestant expression associated with the Great Religious Awakenings in the United States, which the establishment of the Jewish state had awakened. Indeed, throughout Jewish history, there has always been a close relationship between messianic expectations and proposals to renew the Sanhedrin.[22] But despite the support of a few prominent religious-Zionist leaders, the proposal itself met with such stiff resistance on the part of most leaders including Chief Rabbi Herzog that it was dropped. Indeed, Herzog's objection may have led some of the proposal's passive adherents to maintain their silence.

Finally, the most radical solution of all was proposed by Moshe Unna, the ideological leader of the religious kibbutz movement. Unna sought to bypass the rabbinate entirely.[23] He argued, and he had proof texts and history to buttress his argument, that religious authority resides in the public as well as in its *halakhic* authorities. Of course, if religious authority resided in the public, presumably the observant public, in what that public wanted and in how that public behaved, its spokesmen were, by definition, its political representatives. In other words, Unna was imbuing the political representatives of religious-Zionism with religious authority and empowering them to introduce the kinds of changes that would satisfy the religious public. Besides a few isolated individuals, only the religious kibbutz movement was prepared to accept this solution. Like the previous solution, the surprise is not that it failed. The surprise is that it was even proposed; pointing once again to the sense of some in those tumultuous days of how almost all things were possible.

The solution that religious-Zionism found to its dilemma of mediating the tension between modernity and tradition, between democracy and *halakha*, between the vision of a Torah state and the inability to operationalize that vision without radically restructuring Jewish law and/or the nature of a democratic polity is the solution that we live with today. It was to retain the slogan of a Torah state, continue to pay lip service to the compatibility of a democratic state and the Jewish tradition, and make no concerted effort to do anything about it. Not surprisingly, the outburst of messianic expectations following Israeli victories in the Six Day War of 1967, led to new efforts in this realm but this is another story.

To return to the earlier period, the transformation of the idea of a Torah state from a program to a slogan appears to be the coward's way out and it may well have been so. But it was probably the wisest course to follow. In Israel, as has been argued elsewhere,[24] the exigencies of governing a state and the constraints of the political system have led the religious parties, *haredi* as well as religious-Zionist to incorporate, quite unselfconsciously new elements and new modes of thinking, and is leading, unselfconsciously we believe, to new categories of *halakhic* thought. Israel, of course, is not a Torah state and is unlikely to ever be one, but many changes that such a state would have introduced into Jewish law, are, slowly, albeit with serious obstacles and temporary retreats, now being realized. Examples include: the democratization of religious parties, even *haredi* parties; the increased role of women in religious life; a more egalitarian image of women in the minds of religious women themselves, of religious men and even among *halakhic* authorities; changed expectations of the religious public with regard to their obligations toward the non-religious; and the changed role of the *haredi* press. We are inclined to believe that continued focus on the provisions of a Torah state would have undermined rather than advanced these developments.

ENDNOTES

1. For a range of views as to the meaning of religious-Zionism, by its proponents, see Yosef Tirosh (ed.), *Religious Zionism: An Anthology* (Jerusalem: The World Zionist Organization, Department for Torah Education and Culture in the Diaspora, 1975).
2. On the historical distinction between religious-Zionists and non-religious Zionists i.e., the *haredim*, often referred to as ultra-Orthodox, see Ehud Luz, *Parallels Meet: Religion and Nationalism in the Early Zionist Movement 1882–1904* (Philadelphia: Jewish Publication Society, 1988).
3. On the importance of the unity of the Jewish people as a cardinal principle of religious-Zionism see Luz, *ibid.* and Aryei Fishman, "Tradition and Innovation Within Religious Zionism," in Avraham Rubinstein (ed.), *Bishvilei Ha'thiya* (Ramat-Gan: Bar-Ilan University Press, in Hebrew, 1983), pp. 127– 147.
4. The most prominent forerunners of modern Zionism were rabbis Zvi Hirsch Kalischer (1795–1874) and Yehuda Alkalai (1798–1878). See Arthur Hertzberg, *The Zionist Idea* (New York: Harper and Row, 1959).
5. On the nature of this earliest wave of immigrants see Mordechai Eliav, *Eretz Israel and its Yishuv in the 19th Century* (Jerusalem: Keter Publishing House, in Hebrew, 1978). On the relationship between the new immigrants and the older settlement of religious Jews in Palestine see Yehoshua Kaniel, "The Old Yishuv and the New Settlements," in Mordechai Eliav (ed.), *Sefer Ha'Aliya Ha'Rishona* (Jerusalem: Yad Yitzhak Ben-Zvi, in Hebrew, 1981), pp. 269–288.
6. On the founding of Mizrachi see David Vital, *Zionism: The Formative Years* (Oxford: Oxford University Press, 1982).
7. On this point see, Charles S. Liebman and Eliezer Don-Yehiya, *Religion and Politics in Israel* (Bloomington: Indiana University Press, 1984), p. 67 and for more elaborate treatment Eliezer Don-Yehiya, "Ideology and Policy: Rabbi Reines' Conception of Zionism and Mizrachi's Stand on the Uganda Issue," *Sugiyot B'Toldot Ha'Tziyonut V'Ha'Yishuv* (Tel Aviv: Am Oved, in Hebrew, 1989), pp. 55–68.
8. See Menachem Friedman, "The Chief Rabbinate — A Dilemma Without A Solution," *Medina, Mimshal V'Yahasim Beynleumiyim* no. 3 (1972), pp. 118–128.
9. Shlomo Zalman Shragai, *T'humim* (in Hebrew, 1952), p. 434.
10. See, for example, Shimon Federbush, *Mishpat Ha'M'lukha B'Yisrael* (Jerusalem: Mosad Harav Kook, in Hebrew, 1952), pp. 7–8; or speeches by Moshe Unna and Shlomo Kahana at the conference of Hapoel Hamizrachi held in 1950, (*Din V'Heshbon shel Ha'V'ida Ha'Asirit shel Histadrut Hapoel*

Hamizrachi (Jerusalem: Histadrut Hapoel Hamizrachi, in Hebrew, 1950), pp. 76 and 114.

11. See, for example, articles in the religious-Zionist newspaper *Hazofe* by Naftali Bar-Giora (August 29, 1947) and Moshe Zvi Neria (January 9, 1948).

12. Aryei Fishman, *Judaism and Modernization on the Religious Kibbutz* (Cambridge: Cambridge University Press, 1992).

13. These and other statements are to be found in the posthumously published papers of Herzog, edited by Itamar Wahrhaftig, which appeared, in Hebrew, under the title A Constitution for Israel According to the Torah. Isaac Herzog, *T'huka L'Yisrael al pi Ha'Torah* (Jerusalem: Mosad Harav Kook — Yad Harav Herzog, in Hebrew, 1989). This particular quote is found in vol. I, p. 19.

14. See, for example, his vigorous intercession in favor of exempting yeshiva students from the draft even in the difficult days of Israel's war of independence. See Menachem Friedman, "And This is the Origin of the Status-Quo: Religion and the State of Israel," Varda Pilovsky (ed.), *Ha'Ma'avar Mi'Yishuv L'Medina 1947–1949* (Haifa: Mosad Herzl L'Heker Ha'Tziyonut, Haifa University, in Hebrew, 1988), pp. 47–79.

15. See Itamar Wahrhaftig's introduction to volume two of *T'huka L'Yisrael al pi HaTorah*, p. 29.

16. The quote is from a letter of Rabbi Isser Unterman, then chief rabbi of Tel-Aviv, later to become Herzog's successor as Ashkenazi chief Rabbi in *ibid.*, p. 183.

17. *Ibid.*, vol. I, p. 229.

18. *Din V'Heshbon shel Ha'V'ida Ha'Olamit Hyod-het shel Hamizrachi* (Jerusalem: 1949), p. 28.

19. *Ibid.*, pp. 124–125.

20. See, for example, Y.L. Hacohen Maimon, "On the Origins of the Idea of Renewing the Sanhedrin," *Sinai*, vol. 30 (1952), "A Speech I Never Gave," *Sinai*, vol. 31 (1952), p. 130; or *Din V'Heshbon ... Hapoel Hamizrachi*, pp. 109–110.

21. On the relationship between religious-Zionism and the chief rabbinate and the different relationships between spiritual and political leaders among *haredim* on the one hand and religious-Zionists on the other see, Eliezer Don-Yehiya, "Religious Leadership and Political Leadership," Ella Belfer (ed.), *Manhigut Ruhanit B'Yisrael* (Jerusalem: D'vir, in Hebrew, 1982), pp. 104– 134.

22. Aviezer Ravitzky, *Ha'ketz Ha'Meguleh U'Medinat Ha'Yehudim* (Tel-Aviv: Am Oved, in Hebrew, 1993), p. 127.

23. See *Din V'Heshbon ... Hapoel Hamizrachi*, pp. 77–78.

24. Charles S. Liebman, "Jewish Fundamentalism and the Israeli Polity," Martin E. Marty and R. Scott Appleby (eds.), *Fundamentalisms and the State* (Chicago: University of Chicago Press, 1992), pp. 68–87.

THREE

A Case of Fundamentalism in Contemporary Israel

Charles S. Liebman and Asher Cohen

The previous chapter suggested that there are basic divisions between *haredim* (ultra-Orthodox, hostile to modernity and anti-Zionist) and religious-Zionists, characterized, at least until recently, by a benevolent attitude toward modernity, and a more permissive attitude toward religious in addition to an affirmation of Zionism.[1] However within each of these camps are sub-groups. Their animosity toward one another (at least among the *haredim*), sometimes leads to outbreaks of violence. Furthermore, the standard division of Orthodox Israelis into the *haredi* and religious-Zionist camps is complicated by the growing religio-political strength of religious oriental Jews — Jews who were born or whose parents were born in Arab speaking countries. They don't fit neatly in either camp. On the other hand one can also point to a growing consensus among all the Orthodox with regard to some major issues.

A few decades ago, this was not true. Aryei Fishman has shown how the religious-Zionists integrated both Zionism and modernity into their religious formulations.[2] But the mood of moderation, openness to new ideas and an emphasis on the universalist dimension of Judaism no longer predominates within religious-Zionist circles in Israel. Instead, a new form of ultra-nationalist religious radicalism has gained increasing ascendancy. Among *haredim*, on the other hand, ultra-nationalist ideals, phrased in religious rather than Zionist terminology, are expressed with increasing frequency. In many respects, therefore, the two religious strands are converging. This convergence is not evident in the assertions of the extremists and ideological purists in either camp but rather in its effect on the larger population of religious Jews who were heretofore identifiable as either *haredi* or religious-Zionist. Today, one can point to the emergence of new groups and/or changes in the ideology of established religious parties which integrate *both* strands.

Support for this approach is found in the growing usage of a label that was invented, over a decade ago — *haredi-leumi* (a nationalist *haredi*). The term was first used by a moderate, anti-*haredi* leader of the religious-Zionist youth movement, Bnei Akiva. He was very concerned with the growth of *haredi* tendencies within his movement, the denigration of secular education in particular, and unhappy, though perhaps less distressed, by the emergence of ultra-nationalist tendencies as well. The term *haredi-leumi* was certainly intended as a term of opprobrium. The term is now born with pride by a growing number of religious schools, by a rapidly growing religious youth movement, Ezra, and by an increasing number of religious Jews who, according to a poll conducted by the religious weekly *Erev Shabbat*, decline to identify themselves as either *haredi* or religious-Zionist but prefer to be called *haredi leumi*.

The growth of *haredi* parties and their ability to attract voters from non-*haredi* segments of the population has been accompanied, at the ideological no less than the pragmatic level, by their *de facto* adoption of a nationalistic orientation and the muting of their ideological objections to Zionism[3] although this tendency does not encompass all *haredim*. Moreover, even where the *haredi* parties adopt a more dovish position on foreign policy issues than does the NRP (the political arm of the religious-Zionists), it reflects pragmatic considerations, coalition arrangements or the hope of securing more government funding for party projects. There is no affirmation among *haredim* about any basic or ultimate rights of the non-Jew, especially with regard to the Land of Israel. Indeed, surveys to which we allude in chapter four indicate that *haredim* are less tolerant of Arab rights than are religious-Zionists.

The theoretical issue dividing *haredi* and religious nationalists is whether or not Jews in Israel are still living under conditions of exile. The *haredim* claim that in a metaphysical sense the Jews still live in exile. This leads some of their leaders, the elders in particular, to feel that Jews ought to behave toward non-Jews with deference lest they irritate them and arouse their always latent feeling of antisemitism. Jews must acknowledge that their own power is inadequate to overcome gentile animus. But there is no question that the animus exists.

Since the beginning of time, there is an undertone of hatred between the Jew and the gentile. Either the gentile hates the Jew or the Jew hates the gentile. It is like a law of nature that is part of the laws of creation; just as there is light in the day and darkness at night.[4]

At the religious-Zionist end of the continuum, the National Religious Party and its constituents, heretofore characterized by religious moderation, by an accommodationist rather than a rejectionist orientation toward modernity and secular culture, shows increasing signs of rejecting modernity and asserting a rather reactionary interpretation of the religious tradition. This is evident in the increased allocation of school time to study of sacred text in religious-Zionist schools, in increasing insistence upon separating the sexes in institutions identified with religious-Zionism and in the increased emphasis on religious observance by many religious-Zionists. Whereas the National Religious Party's platform on the future of the territories has been increasingly radicalized and now virtually mirrors that of the radical right, it, and other institutions of the religious-Zionist camp adopt positions in other matters which increasingly resemble those of the *haredim*. Thus, the counterpart to the nationalization of the *haredim* is the *haredization* of the religious-Zionists.

In summary, the argument presented here is that there is less point today than there was in the past in distinguishing among the segments of religious Jewry, for purposes of assessing their relationship to democratic ideas and structures within Israeli society. This does not mean that all religious Jewry or all the religious parties are cut of one cloth. There are different orientations which one can distinguish among parties, among groups within the different parties and among individual political and religious leaders. Nor have differences between *haredim* and religious-Zionists entirely disappeared. But mainstream currents among religious-Zionists as well as *haredim* are becoming increasingly similar. Whether it is proper to label them as fundamentalist is another question. In some respects it is a matter of definition, a matter to which we now turn our attention.

Use of the term fundamentalist often fails to distinguish between fundamentalism and religious seriousness. The two terms are often confused, especially by secularists in academia and the media, and by religious liberals. Whether they do so from bad faith or ignorance is hard to know. But it is clear that they tend to apply the term fundamentalist to all those who don't share their point of view.

We want to clarify what we mean by a religiously serious position and then describe, using the example of Jewish ultra-nationalists, conceptions or orientations relevant to religion and politics which fundamentalists *share* with religiously serious people and notions which are *peculiar* to fundamentalists.

There is a problem in applying the label "fundamentalist" to any group of Jews. The term "fundamentalism" arose in association with American Protestantism. It recalls the twelve volume work titled *The Fundamentals* published between 1910 and 1915.[5] The term not only originates in the context of American Protestantism but the centrality and interpretation of the doctrine of Biblical inerrancy is peculiarly Protestant.

Biblical inerrancy is a fundamental belief of Judaism. But it plays a very different role in Judaism than in Protestantism. Protestantism encourages the individual to engage in an unmediated reading of the text whereas Judaism is built upon a "tradition" of biblical commentary and homily. One of the spiritual leaders of the ultra-nationalist religious-Zionists, all of whom approach, in varying degree, the fundamentalist end of the continuum to be described below, states what virtually every Jewish religious leader would affirm:

The Torah has seventy faces and everyone has the right to explain any line in scripture according to his understanding ... The question therefore arises: who decides what is the correct interpretation ...? The answer is: tradition.[6]

Since it is the tradition rather than the text itself which is central to one's understanding of God's demands, biblical inerrancy, although a cardinal tenet of belief, is secondary rather than central in Jewish theology.

Nevertheless, the term fundamentalism has assumed new meanings in current discussion. It has been divorced from its historical Protestant association. In the popular media it seems to refer to a movement or group which is very zealous in its religious belief and seeks to do something very radical in the social and political realm as a consequence of this belief. A vast scholarly literature has emerged in the last decade which also recognizes fundamentalism as an orientation that cuts across all major religions.[7] It seems to me that there are three major characteristics of fundamentalism that cross religious boundaries and enable us to include Judaism under its rubric. Fundamentalists conceive of their religion as: 1) totalistic, it is related to all aspects of life, 2) exclusivistic, it rejects all claims to ultimate truth other than its own, and 3) precise or certain; the adherent is able to fully understand the truths which the religion affirms in the sense that he/she knows what God wants.

Totalism and exclusivism are related. To argue that one's religion or the truth contained in one's religion is exclusivistic implies that it is totalistic as well. Otherwise, truths from other areas of life might overlap religious truths. But we want to stress the third characteristic of fundamentalism, one that has received less scholarly attention — the attribute of certainty. Insofar as the fundamentalist is concerned, God's revelation, whether it is direct, or through scripture, or through authoritative interpretations of scripture, expresses in clear straightforward terms how the individual and society ought to behave and what one ought to believe. One is, therefore, *certain* about the content of the message.

Our argument is that within each of the major religions, or at least each of the Abrahamic religions, one may construct a conceptual continuum along which individuals and groups can be ranged in accordance with the degree to which religion governs their lives. Religious liberals stand at one end of the continuum. Liberals tend to interpret their religious obligations in a manner which accords with notions of ethics, propriety and self-interest that are derived, consciously as well as unconsciously, from non-religious sources. In addition, the scope of religious obligations tends to be minimized rather than maximized. In other words, religion is neither totalistic or exclusivistic and religious liberals are not certain about anything in the religious realm other than their certainty that non-liberals are wrong.

Further along the continuum are those whom we identify as religiously serious but non-fundamentalist. Like the liberals, they also interpret religion in accordance with notions of ethics, propriety and self-interest which are derived from non-religious sources (the process is inevitable), but they do so unconsciously rather than consciously. Not from choice but as part of the dynamics of life. To the extent they are aware of this, it troubles them. Religiously serious individuals affirm a God and a tradition which stands outside the individual. Religious obligations and conceptions of reality are conceived of as imposed from without, in an objective manner — not as the consequence of the subjective understanding and experience of the religious adherent.

At the extreme end of the continuum are the fundamentalists who share all the characteristics of the religiously serious but are more committed to the principles of totalism and exclusivism, more sensitive to excising concepts of ethics, propriety and self-interest derived from non-religious sources (though they are likely to fail in this regard). But most characteristic of the fundamentalist, and peculiar to fundamentalism as we define the phenomenon, is the notion of certainty. Fundamentalists are certain they know what God wants of them. However, even among fundamentalists one finds degrees of certainty.

All religiously serious people, including, of cause, fundamentalists, share the belief that God revealed himself and continues to reveal himself — not only in sacred text but in the course of history and in events which we experience. It follows, therefore, that both history and the events we experience teach us something about what God wants of us. This doesn't necessarily mean that we can interpret history or the events we experience without the assistance of sacred text, or the guidance of sages who are learned in religious lore, or clerics who possess charismatic authority. The identity of the religious authority varies among different religious traditions and among schools of thought or movements within particular religious traditions. But, common to all these traditions is the conviction that God's will is to be found, among other places, in our world.

Anyone familiar with the Bible will recognize the roots of this tradition. But it has a logically compelling quality as well. The alternative is to conclude that the course of human history is contrary to God's will or that God is indifferent to what happens in human history. Consequently, religiously serious people will at least consider and assess events to look for signs from God even if, as in Judaism or Islam, they can only be decoded within the context of the textual tradition and/or by those who are learned in sacred text.

The problem arises, as already noted, in decoding God's signs. Heraclitus observed that "The lord whose oracle is in Delphi neither speaks out nor conceals, but gives a sign." The fundamentalists, at least the extremists among them, think He does better than this and it is at this point that they part company from other religiously serious people. Fundamentalists are certain of what contemporary events signify — a belief natural enough in satisfying the need so many of us have for a measure of certainty in our lives. The political consequences, however, are destructive of a stable political system in general and democracy in particular. For as Uriel Tal has observed:

> ... the dilemma of political theology may be summed up as follows: if religion is to be conscientiously relevant, it must be involved in socio-political life ... Since the authority of religion is divine, and thus absolute, introducing religion into socio-political affairs frequently brings about the absolute sacralization of those affairs.[8]

One escape from this dilemma is to deny certainty. Indeed, in contrast to the fundamentalists who are certain of God's signs, the mainstream Jewish tradition urges the faithful to search for the meaning of events with no assurance that they will succeed. The ultimate punishment which God inflicts is *hester panim*, the hiding of God's face so that one no longer receives or can interpret God's wish. But in normal times, we assume that signs exist and Jews are commanded to search for their meaning.

The Jewish tradition speaks more of the signs signalled by tragedy rather than by the signs signaled by success or victory. The Bible warns Jews against believing that their success is the outcome of their own efforts. Success is a sign of God's favor but one is unclear about why that favor was granted. National calamity, on the other hand, always follows from national sin and Jews are instructed to search for the sin. At the very least, they are urged to "repent". This demand, invariably uttered by traditional religious leaders in the wake of some collective disaster, is more than a meaningless formula. Because there is an alternative interpretation to calamity. Suffering can also be understood as a mode of purification and a signal of imminent redemption. In the hands of messianists, those who look for signs of the coming of the Messiah and total Redemption, defeat and the attendant suffering can become powerful vehicles for mobilizing a population to anticipate divine redemption. Following the 1973 Yom Kippur War, Rav Shach, the preeminent leader of the ultra-Orthodox Jewish world attacked messianic tendencies within both the ultra-Orthodox as well as the religious-Zionist world.[9] The suffering invoked by the Yom Kippur War, he stressed, is a sign to Jews that they must repent of their sins and become religiously observant. Those who argue that this is the suffering that precedes Redemption, according to Rav Shach, were distorting the true message of the War and misleading Jews about their obligation to repent.

Rav Shach's interpretation of the meaning of collective suffering characterizes the Jewish tradition's attitude toward personal tragedy as well. Individual tragedy and suffering may be the consequence of a number of factors. Jews are instructed to examine themselves for their sins so they may repent of them. But there is no assurance that a particular personal tragedy is a punishment for the sufferer's own sins. It may be punishment for someone else's sins but it may also be a sign that the sufferer is peculiarly righteous. Doubt may linger in the mind of the sufferer himself and will certainly linger in the mind of others.

It would seem to follow that if national calamity is a punishment for collective sins, national success is a reward for collective virtue. This is certainly true in the case of Islam where the notion of success as a reward for virtue plays a more central role than it does in Judaism. It is not entirely absent in Judaism, and it would be most unnatural if it were. But the messianic dimension serves as a balance. This requires some explanation.

Jews are assured that the Messiah, the descendent of David, will come some day. This, according to the Jewish view, is the ultimate Redemption. A number of events will occur when the Messiah comes. They include the gathering of Jews from the "four corners of the earth" to the land of Israel. In addition, the Temple will be rebuilt or miraculously reappear on Mount Zion, the Temple Mount where two major Muslim shrines now stand. But these events needn't occur in the first stage of Redemption. There are differences of opinion as to how one can identify the Messiah or precisely what else will happen when he does come. But a central pillar of Judaism is the notion that the coming of the Messiah is associated with Redemption bringing an end to the trials and tribulations which have been the lot of the Jews since their exile. There are also different opinions within the tradition as to the conditions under which the Messiah will come. In fact, according to some, he will come to a generation that is totally bereft of spiritual virtue. In accordance with this view, Redemption is not necessarily due to the virtues of the Jews. Events in this world may signal Redemption, and such events would be cause for great gladness. But they are not necessarily the outcome of Jewish virtue. Jewish victory or success may presage the coming of Redemption without necessarily testifying to the virtues of the Jews who enjoy that victory or success.

Does any victory or success presage Redemption? Unlikely. Victory or success cannot be understood as signalling Redemption unless it is of truly astounding proportions. Of course, whether an event is or is not "astounding" is essentially one of perception. An astounding event is one which is perceived as astounding.

To some Jews the most astounding event of the modern period was the "emancipation". The "emancipation" refers to the civil and religious freedoms which Jews began to enjoy in eighteenth and nineteenth century Europe. These freedoms were accompanied by an expectation, among wealthier Jews in particular, that complete political and economic freedom as well as social equality was likely to follow. Since the Jewish tradition affirms the continuous hatred of the Gentile for the Jew, a condition which is part of the very nature of the Gentile and the rhythms of the world, the willingness of the Gentile to free the Jew of economic and political disabilities signaled a cataclysmic change in the nature of the world. One could hardly expect a religious Jew not to see the hand of God in this change. Emancipation, therefore, was perceived by a few Jewish leaders as so astounding an event as to signal the beginning of Redemption.[10] Subsequent events such as the Balfour Declaration of 1917 in which Great Britain promised to assist in the establishment of a Jewish commonwealth in Palestine, and the establishment of the

State of Israel in 1948 were interpreted by many religious Jews in this light.[11] These interpretations were not inconsistent with one another. Redemption is not a short term event but may extend over a considerable length of time. Aryei Fishman observes that the messianic echoes which the political emancipation and the national rebirth evoked were expressed in three interdependent channels: recognition of the present as a period of distinctive religious meaning, a positive attitude toward the world and humanity in general, and a world view which allowed for rational Jewish behavior in order to facilitate the coming of the Messiah.[12] The time was ripe, in other words, in the eyes of God, for Jews not only to anticipate but to act in order to hasten Redemption.

The growing certainty about imminent Redemption reached new heights following the Six Day War of June 1967. The "miraculous" victory of the Jews, in which they not only avoided destruction but captured territories which had clear religious associations (the Old City of Jerusalem containing the Western Wall, the Temple Mount, and Mount Olives, and the cities of Hebron, Shechem ((Nablus)), and Jericho, all with powerful biblical associations) seemed to many religious Jews a clear demonstration that those visionaries who saw the beginning of Redemption more than one hundred years earlier had been correct. Here, for example, is a how one rabbi, known for his moderate posture in social and political matters, someone whom we would describe as religiously serious but not a fundamentalist, framed the issue:

> ... most thinking Jewish people agree that the events of the past hundred or 120 years beginning with the first stirrings of the Jewish national movements — ... culminating in the Six-Day War — could be seen, without falling into the trap of pseudo-Messianism, as a historically well-attested movement towards *Ge'ulah* [Redemption]. And while each one separately could be considered a flash in the pan, taken together in their historical, almost logical, sequence, nobody, as rational as he might be, could be blamed for seeing the hand of God in what happened.[13]

A more fundamentalist like position, one that involves greater certainty about the timing of the Redemption process, is expressed by Rav Zvi Yehuda Kook (1891–1982), the spiritual leader of the religious ultra-nationalists:

> People speak of "the dawn of the Redemption". In my opinion we are in the midst of Redemption. The dawn took place a hundred years ago. We are in the parlor, not the hallway.[14]

The gap between the ultra-nationalist fundamentalists and the main camp of religious Zionists in Israel grew in the aftermath of the 1973 Yom Kippur war. For the question now became, how was one to interpret what Israelis perceived as their defeat in that war? One might argue that the Yom Kippur War was not an Israeli defeat but that is not how Israeli society interprets that war[15] and this is not the place to elaborate upon the reasons or adequacy of that interpretation. Under these circumstances how was one to interpret it? Non-fundamentalist were in somewhat of a quandary. A symposium following the Yom Kippur War brought together a range of religious educators. Some of them might be described as fundamentalists, others not. In his opening remarks, the chairman, Michael Rosenak, introduced the topic in a manner typical of the religiously serious non-fundamentalist:

> ... we have tended in the recent past, especially after the Six-Day War, to ascribe unambiguous significance to great events, especially wars. In point of fact, significance is to be sought not only in wars or other great events but also in everyday life. Nevertheless ... while we cannot ascribe significance to events in the same way that prophets would and did, we are called upon to react and act as educators, citizens and as Jews, even if we hesitate about the way we are going to do so.[16]

Other, however, expressed less uncertainty. Demurring from the chairman's remarks, Rabbi Eliezer Waldman, spiritual leader of an educational institution located in the heart of the West Bank and one who was later elected to the Knesset as a representative of an ultra-nationalist party, said:

> I disagree ... that when there are difficulties and suffering, one does not see the progress of *Ge'ulah* [Redemption] clearly; this is not because there are no steps

forward, but because there is one step backward in order to take two steps forward ... our way is marked by constant struggle. If some say "Let redemption come but I don't wish to see it" it is because of the difficulties and suffering which will accompany it ... we do not seek suffering, we prefer to do without it, but we know that suffering cleanses.[17]

This is consistent with Gideon Aran's comment that among the religious ultra-nationalists the suffering which the war inflicted was interpreted as:

... the "pangs of the Messiah," the trials and tribulations which emerge before redemption, heralding and conditioning its fulfillment.[18]

A more extreme fundamentalist position (extreme because of its certainty about the nature of the Jews' sin) explained the war as punishment for the collective sin of the Jews who did not settle and annex the holy land which God had given to them in the miraculous victory of the Six Day War. International pressure for:

... withdrawal from the territories in the wake of a cruel war is a crucible, a trial in which God tests Israel ...[19]

This rational can be carried one step further to the most extreme conclusion. If one can anticipate what God will do in the future, one can manipulate God. Knowing what God will's Himself to do, one can force Him to do what the believer wants.

This strategy has been tellingly described, though not in these terms, in a recent book by Robert Bartlett, *Trial By Fire and Water*.[20] In medieval Christendom, trial by ordeal was not uncommon when the evidence was inconclusive. Bartlett points out that whereas the idea originated with Germanic tribes, it was spread by the Church from 915 until it was denounced by Pope Innocent III in 1215 whereupon it was generally abandoned. The theological basis for the ordeal seems straight forward enough. If a human court does not know whether a suspected criminal is guilty or not guilty, the suspect might undergo, sometimes voluntarily and sometimes involuntarily an ordeal — generally by either fire or water. The ordeal by fire involved the suspect seizing or walking upon a hot iron rod. Judges would examine the hand or foot of the accused after a period of time to see if it had healed. The logic behind the ordeal was that God would intervene to demonstrate the innocence or guilt of the suspected party. The rituals for the hot iron, Bartlett notes, frequently contained the invocation "If you are innocent of this charge ... you may confidently receive this iron in your hand and the Lord, the just judge, will free you, just as he snatched the three children from the burning fire."[21] Furthermore, the signs had to be unambiguous, since it was the court, i.e. human beings who would interpret them.

The theological basis of the trial by ordeal is echoed in the activity of a small group of extreme Jewish fundamentalists. In 1984 a number of Israelis identified with Gush Emunim (the group of ultra-nationalist mostly religious Jews who settled the West Bank, sometimes in violation of Israeli law), were arrested and charged with having engaged and/or planned to engage in a series of violent acts including murder. Although the group were identified in the public mind as "the underground", and although the members knew one another, not all of them were privy to all the illegal acts which members of the group performed or planned. A handful of defendants were charged with plotting to blow up the two Muslim holy places, the Dome of the Rock and the Al Aksa mosque located on the Temple Mount.

The Temple Mount is, in Judaism, the most sacred spot of the universe, the navel of the world, the *axis mundi*. It is the site of the first two Temples and the site where, Jews believe, the third Temple will be located after the coming of the Messiah. Yet, in 1967, when the Israeli army captured the old city of Jerusalem which includes the Temple Mount, they left the Muslim structures untouched — indeed, they permitted Moslem religious authorities to retain control over the Temple Mount. According to some ultra-nationalist fundamentalists, this was a grave religious sin. The punishment for that sin, in their mind, was the 1978 peace agreement with Egypt in which Israel surrendered territory (holy land) that had been captured in the Six Day War. The peace agreement, in their view was, in the words of one scholar:

A direct signal from heaven that a major national offense was committed, a sin that was responsible for the political disaster and its immense spiritual consequences. Only one prominent act of desecration could match the magnitude of the setback: the presence of the Muslims and their shrine on Temple Mount, the holiest Jewish site, the sacred place of the first, second and third (future) temples.[22]

Hence, a handful of zealots conceived the idea of blowing up the Moslem holy places. This act, they believed would do more than please God. It would, as one scholar, based on his discussions with the leader of the plot explains:

... trigger the transformation of the state of Israel from one system of laws to another. It was meant to elevate the nation *now* to the status of the kingdom of Israel, a kingdom of priests capable of actualizing the laws of destiny and of changing the nature of the world.[23]

This process would have been inevitable. By implication, at least, since Israel would have been behaving in accordance with its destiny, God, as it were, would have had no choice in the matter. This is what we mean by coercing God. Others have also understood the intent to blow up the Temple Mount as an effort to coerce God, but in more explicit terms. According to one version, the act would have incited a Moslem holy war against the Jews and Israel — a holy war in which God would be obliged to intervene on behalf of the Jews and thereby hasten the final stages of the Redemption.[24]

The notions of trial by ordeal and the conviction about the consequences of purging the Temple Mount of Moslem "abominations" stem from a certainty about the meaning of God's signs and, at least implicitly, that human beings can coerce God. It suggests that God is not omnipotent since he is constrained by his own plans. It virtually asserts the omniscience of man, or at least that group of men who are capable of knowing these plans in their detail. In this respect it is peculiarly homocentric. But in another respect it is highly mechanistic suggesting that not only God but all other humans respond in preordained ways to events over which they have no control. These notions about God and man are not without basis within the biblical and later rabbinical tradition. The Jewish tradition is a rich one and it bears many strains and echoes of alternative beliefs and conceptions. But this one certainly runs counter to the main thrust of the tradition. Indeed, it is significant that as the church debated trial by ordeal, its proponents were unable to cite clear biblical precedent and its opponents seized on this weakness.[25] The more characteristic attitude of the tradition is reflected in the Book of Judith. In that story, the town of Bethulia is under siege and the townspeople beseech their leader to surrender. He urges them to hold out for five days longer and if God will not help them within that period of time the town will surrender despite the disastrous consequences this would have, from a strategic point of view, for Jerusalem and the rest of Judea. Judith, heroine of the Book, issues the following reproach:

> Listen to me, rulers of the inhabitants of Bethulia, for the thing is not right that you have said before the people today, and have confirmed with this oath that you have sworn between God and you, saying that you will surrender the town to our enemies, unless the Lord turns and helps us within that time. Now who are you, who have tried God today, and who set yourselves up in place of God among the sons of men? ... For if he does not wish to help us within these five days, he has power to protect us within whatever time he pleases, or to destroy us before our enemies. But you must not treat the counsels of the Lord our God as pledged, for God is not like a man, to be threatened, or like a son of man to be cajoled. Therefore let us wait for the deliverance that comes from him, and call upon him to help us, and he will hear our cry, if it pleases him.[26]

An old Jewish joke was reformulated by England's chief rabbi Dr. Jonathan Sacks in contemporary terms. He tells of the pious Jew, living in a sea side community threatened by flood. Residents were called upon to evacuate their homes but the pious Jew refused, expressing his confidence that God would save him. A rescue team came by as the water level rose but the pious Jew still declared that he would not leave — that God would save him. As the water continued to rise the Jew climbed to the second story. A row boat came by with an offer of help but the Jew repeated his confidence that God would save him. Finally, he had to climb to the roof of his home. A passing helicopter threw down a ladder but the pious Jew refused this offer as well. He drowned. Befitting his piety, he went directly to heaven. Storming into the celestial chamber he demanded to know why God had done nothing to save him. "But I did," answered the sovereign of the universe, "I sent you a rescue team, a row boat and a helicopter".

We believe this comes closer to expressing traditional Jewish theology than do the formulations of the extreme fundamentalists.

ENDNOTES

1. The most comprehensive work on contemporary *haredi* society in Israel is Menachem Friedman, *The Haredi (Ultra-Orthodox) Society — Sources, Trends and Processes* (Jerusalem: The Jerusalem Institute for Israel Studies, in Hebrew, 1991).
2. Aryei Fishman, " 'Torah and Labor': The Radicalization of Religion within a National Framework," *Studies in Zionism*, no. 6 (August, 1982), pp. 255–271; "Tradition and Renewal In the Religious-Zionist Experience," Abraham Rubinstein (ed.), *In the Paths of Renewal: Studies in Religious Zionism* (Ramat-Gan: Bar-Ilan University Press, in Hebrew, 1983), pp. 127–147; and Fishman's introduction and the collection of documents in *Hapoel Hamizrachi: 1921–1935* (Tel-Aviv: Tel-Aviv University, in Hebrew, 1979).
3. Yosef Fund, *Agudat Israel Confronting Zionism and the State of Israel — Ideology and Policy* (Bar-Ilan University, Ph.D. dissertation, in Hebrew, 1989).
4. Aharon Sorsky, "You Have Chosen Us From Amongst All the Nations," *Diglenu* (Sivan, 1974, in Hebrew), p. 6.
5. George M. Marsden, *Fundamentalism and American Culture* (New York: Oxford University Press, 1980).
6. Shlomo Aviner, *Shalhevetyah* (Jerusalem: Seder Beyn Hahomot, in Hebrew, 1989), p. 143).
7. One of the most ambitious efforts in this regard is the fundamentalism project of the American Academy of Arts and Sciences. This is a series of volumes edited by Martin Marty and Scott Appleby published by the University of Chicago Press.

8. Uriel Tal, "Totalitarian Democratic Hermeneutics and Policies in Modern Jewish Religious Nationalism," The Israel Academy of Sciences and Humanities, *Totalitarian Democracy and After* (Jerusalem: The Magnes Press, 1984), p. 157.

9. Rav Shach's message is reprinted in *Yated Ne'eman*, the Hebrew language newspaper which accepts his unquestioned authority. See the supplement, "The Weekly Yated" (October 3, 1990), p. 16.

10. See, for example, Jacob Katz, "Israel and the Messiah," reprinted in Jacob Katz, *Jewish Emancipation and Self Emancipation* (Philadelphia: Jewish Publication Society, 1986), p. 157.

11. Aviezer Ravitzky, "Exile in the Holy Land: The Dilemma of Haredi Jewry," Peter Medding (ed.), *Israel State and Society, 1948–1988 Studies in Contemporary Jewry: An Annual V* (New York: Oxford University Press, 1989), pp. 89–125.

12. Aryei Fishman, *Between Religion and Ideology* (Jerusalem: Yad Yitzhak Ben-Zvi, in Hebrew, 1990), p. 24.

13. Alexander Carlebach in "The Yom Kippur War and Its Aftermath," *Niv Hamidrashia*, 11, "English Section," 1974, p. 10.

14. Cited in Shimon Federbush (ed.), *Torah U'M'lukha* (Jerusalem: Mossad Harav Kook, in Hebrew, 1971). p. 102.

15. Charles S. Liebman, "The Myth of Defeat: The Memory of the Yom Kippur War in Israeli Society," *Middle Eastern Studies*, 29 (July 1993), pp. 399–418.

16. "The Yom Kippur War and Its Aftermath," *op. cit.*, pp. 7–8.

17. *Ibid.*, pp. 14–15.

18. Gideon Aran, "Jewish Zionist Fundamentalism: The Bloc of the Faithful in Israel (Gush Emunim)," Martin Marty and Scott Appleby (eds.), *Fundamentalism Observed* (Chicago: University of Chicago Press, 1991).

19. *Ibid.*

20. Robert Bartlett, *Ordeal by Fire and Water: The Medieval Judicial Ordeal* (New York: Oxford University Press, 1986).

21. *Ibid.*, p. 21. The reference is to Hanania, Mishael and Azaria who are mentioned in the biblical Book of Daniel. Within the Jewish tradition, the miraculous escape of the three from the fiery oven in which they were thrown was a result of their special virtues. The *Sefer Ha-hinnukh* is a late 13th century popular work which explains each of the 613 Biblical commandments which Jews are obliged to obey. The book has remained influential to this day in shaping the perceptions of religious Jews. The author, in his commentary to commandment number 546, notes that whereas, "no one raises a finger below [i.e. on earth] unless it has been decreed from above [i.e. by God]" one is nevertheless obliged "to protect oneself from the force of natural events in the world because God created and built the world on the basis of nature and has decreed that fire will burn and water put out fire." Hanania, Mishael and Azaria are cited as exceptions. Because of their righteousness God suspended the laws of nature on their behalf as he did for Daniel. But Jews must never depend on God's doing so. (We are indebted to Professor Moshe Greenberg for bringing this citation to our attention).

22. The summary statement is based on an interview by Ehud Sprinzak with Yehuda Etzion, leader of the conspiracy to blow up the Temple Mount. Ehud Sprinzak, "Fundamentalism, Terrorism, and Democracy: The Case of Gush Emunim Underground," (Washington, D.C.: The Wilson Center, Occasional Paper no. 4, (1986), p. 5.
23. *Ibid.*, p. 14.
24. The attribution of intent to precipitate a holy war in which God would have to intervene was reported in private conversation with Yisrael Eldad in the summer of 1984. Eldad, was a leader of Lehi (the Stern Gang), a terrorist group which fought the British prior to the establishment of the Jewish state. Eldad is one of the few Israelis who publicly advocates terrorism in order to secure political objectives. He was much admired by members of the Jewish underground and although he is not religious, he admired their ideals as well as their courage and applauded most of their acts. He visited them while they were in prison and, in discussion with one of us expressed his dismay at the plan to blow up the Temple Mount. "We in the Lehi," he said, "always considered the consequences of our acts". "What", he went on, "did those who sought to blow up the Temple Mount think would happen?" He then described the scenario to which we alluded in the text. This may stem from a misunderstanding.

A major source for understanding the mentality of the Jewish underground members is a book by one of its members, Haggai Segal, *Dear Brothers: The West Bank Jewish Underground* (Woodmere, N.Y.: Beit-Shamai Publications, 1988). Segal makes it clear that the handful of those involved in the plot to blow up the Temple Mount were motivated by a number of factors. At the simplest most pragmatic level, the act was expected to interrupt the peace process between Israel and Egypt (Segal, pp. 139–140). But religious-messianic motivations were paramount. According to Yehuda Etzion, the architect and ideologue of the plan, purging the Temple Mount was a necessary step in Redemption (Segal, p. 67), but more than that it would have the consequence of "triggering the process", (Segal, p. 316 and Sprinzak, *Ibid.*

There are other allusions to the notion of coercing God. For example, after imprisonment, one of the participants in the Temple Mount plot ruminated that maybe he should have planted the bombs and hooked the fuses without setting them off. "We would have taken care of our part in the sense of mobilizing higher forces by earthly action". (Segal, p. 313). Additional evidence is Segal's comment about Dan Be'eri, an early partner to the plot. According to Segal:

Be'eri's feelings about possible outcomes of the Temple Mount explosion were based in part on the teachings of Rabbi Zvi Yehuda Kook, which allowed the public at large much less room for free choice than the individual. History is not up for grabs, he believed, and if Divine providence does not want the plan to work, it won't work in any case. (p. 136.)

But this still seems to us to fall short of the explicit and conscious effort to coerce God, a charge that even some who shared the political world view of the conspirators leveled. (See, for example, the letter to Etzion cited in Segal, p. 254 and Yitzhak Shilat, "And We Will Renew the Kingdom There," *Hazofeh*, (May 25, 1984), in Hebrew, p. 5. The notion that this act and its consequences would force God to adopt certain measures is not explicit in Etzion's own writings, see for example Yehuda Etzion, "From Laws of Existence to Laws of Destiny" *Nekudah* no. 75 (July 6, 1984), in Hebrew, pp. 22–23, 26–27, nor in Ehud Sprinzak's interviews with Etzion. We believe it unlikely that a fundamentalist ideologue would conceal the basic justification for what he had done although one might argue that to admit to the effort to coerce God is to invite charges of heresy. The charge that Etzion and his collaborators sought to provoke a Moslem *jihad* that would have forced God to intervene and thereby precipitate Redemption is also contrary to Segal's report of his discussions with the conspirators who did not believe that the Moslem world really cared that much.

25. The one arguable exception is when a wife, suspected of infidelity, is subject to the test of bitter waters. For more on this point and its role in the debate over the legitimacy of the ordeal see Bartlett, *op. cit.*, pp. 83–85.

26. *The Apocrypha*, an American translation by Edgar J. Goodspeed (New York: Random House, 1959), pp. 146–147.

FOUR

Democracy and Religion in Israeli Society[1]

In chapter one I described the dilemma which religion poses for democratic societies. Many attitudes which religion imparts are inimicable to democracy. On the other hand, democratic societies need religion in order to sustain the social order. Israel provides a nice illustration of the problem.

Virtually every survey of Israeli Jews concludes that among the more religious segment of the population one finds the least commitment to democratic values, and among the least religious segment of the population one finds the greatest commitment to democratic values.[2] Differences remain when we hold constant for ethnic origin or education and therefore suggest that a religious factor of one kind or another does account, at least in part, for the differences among these population groups.

As chapter one suggests, democratic attitudes or democratic commitment refers to a package of attitudes or values. I don't think that those who have expressed concern about the relative absence of positive attitudes toward democracy among religious Jews (*datiim*, sing. *dati*), have always focussed on the right questions or the important questions. For example, respondents are sometimes asked if they would give greater weight to a decision by the Knesset or a decision by rabbinical authority. This is not an adequate measure of attitudes toward democracy among the religious population for a number of reasons. First, one hopes that all citizens cherish certain principles to which they accord higher value than legislative law. In other words, under certain circumstances every Israeli ought to give greater weight to a moral authority or ethical code outside the elected system of government than to the decisions of any institution within the system. If this leads to a violation of the law, than the imperatives of the democratic system require that a citizen willingly pay the price for violating the law. *Halakha* constitutes a system of morality as well as law for the observant Jew.

Secondly, a religious Jew, by virtue of being a religious Jew, is bound by *halakhic* decisions. This is the essence of a Jew's self-identity as *dati*. Hence, when asked a question about the relative weight he/she would give to a rabbinic decision or a Knesset law, the religious Jew will always answer that greater weight will be given to an *halakhic* decision. Whether, in practice, the *dati* Jew would actually do so is a different matter entirely.

Finally, it is difficult to imagine the circumstances under which the Knesset would pass a law contrary to that which all authoritative rabbinical voices interpreted as Jewish law. In order for such a situation to arise two conditions would have to be met. The Knesset would have to pass such a law with all the consequences involved in deliberately defying the religious tradition, and the religious elite would have to interpret the law as contrary to *halakha* with all the consequences that such a defiance of the authority of the state would entail. In other words, not only would the present political constellation have to change, but the whole climate of attitudes toward Judaism, to be discussed below, would have to change. But let us assume that this did occur. All it would do is establish a situation which is no different, in theory, from a situation that arises when an individual is faced with a contradiction between positive law and his own moral convictions. The democratic system is in no danger as long as this sort of thing doesn't happen too often or too many people don't find the law incompatible with their moral conscience.

A second charge is also leveled against the democratic propensities of the *datiim*. Their support for passage of "religious" legislation is interpreted as an effort at "religious coercion", i.e. the violation of freedom of conscience. It seems to me that this charge is unfair. Much of the legislation which some religious parties, Agudat Yisrael in particular, have proposed may be neither fair nor wise. Such laws may have deleterious economic consequences for particular individuals (such as the prohibition against raising or selling pigs and pork products), or even the entire economy (such as the prohibition of El Al flights on the Sabbath or restricting factories from operating on the Sabbath). In addition, some laws such as those prohibiting bus transportation on the Sabbath is a source of inconvenience, in some cases serious inconvenience to many Israelis. Efforts to restrict abortion may have unfortunate effects on the health of women, although this is by no means assured. But it is wrong to frame the debate over these prohibitions and restrictions in term of democracy and religious conscience. I don't believe, in any event, that this is how the vast majority of Israelis see the issue. The real issue, at least in the eyes of most Israelis, is over the extent to which Israeli public life ought to reflect the Jewish nature of the state and to what extent, in so doing, the state may infringe upon the private rights of individuals.

All of the *dati* parties, including the most extreme, deny that they seek to impose religious law in the private domain, although some, as we shall see, don't object to such infringement in principle. In other words, while some religious parties would welcome a constitutional upheaval which would substitute religious law for Knesset legislation, no *dati* party seeks to generate such an upheaval. In this respect, it is worth noting, they differ from the fundamentalist parties in Islamic countries. Even the most extreme *dati* parties accept, in broad outline, the rules of the democratic system which includes individual liberties and freedoms. On the other hand, virtually all of the political parties in the Knesset who represent Jews rather than Arabs still favor recognizing the Jewish nature of the state in public life in some form or another. As we will see in the next chapter, this is likely to change. But as late as 1985, the Knesset amended the "Basic Law: The Knesset" to prohibit a party from participating in Knesset elections "if its goals, explicitly or implicitly, or its actions include ... negation of the existence of the State of

Israel as the State of the Jewish people." In other words, no political party may challenge the Jewish nature of the state. Israel pays lip service to the notion of the equality of all its citizens under its law[3] but it does not accord national rights to non-Jews.[4] This has much more to do with Zionism than with Judaism. It is a commitment which the overwhelming majority of Israeli Jews share. But it is a mistake to think that commitment to a Jewish state is simply a euphemism for denying Israeli Arabs a right to national assertion. The vast majority of Israeli Jews also believe that Judaism, i.e. the religious tradition, ought to find expression in public life. The debate between the *dati* and non-*dati* parties over issues of religious legislation or religious coercion, therefore, was not, until most recently, framed in terms of a debate over the principle of democracy but over the interpretation of what the Jewish nature of public life means and what the private rights of individuals means. Basic democratic principles are not at stake in this conflict in the sense that having overturned one principle (e.g. freedom of speech or minority rights), all other principles are endangered. Some political liberals prefer to see the conflict in those terms but this distorts the nature of the debate as it takes place in the minds of most of the protagonists. However, in the last few years, especially since the Rabin assasination, those who favor minimizing the Jewish nature of Public life phrase their position in terms of democratic values. I deal with this tension in the final chapter.

Even if we concede that *dati* support for "religious" legislation or their prior commitment to *halakha* over Knesset legislation is not a threat to democracy, the fact remains that *datiim* are more likely than non-*datiim* to favor censorship, restricting criticism of the government and distinguishing between the rights and freedom of Jews and non-Jews, even if the latter are citizens of Israel. These attitudes reflect positions that are shared by Jewish religious leaders, that is by the Jewish establishment, the institutional guardians of Judaism. Whether they actually reflect the position of Judaism is a question of semantics. It depends on whose interpretation of Judaism is authoritative.

RELIGIOUS LEADERS AND DEMOCRACY

Statements by religious spokesmen about democracy generally refer to the formal properties of the system — majority rule and some guarantee of individual rights. Although some religious leaders have interpreted Judaism as incompatible with democracy, others view the two systems as totally harmonious.[5] At the theoretical level there are differences between *haredim* and many religious-Zionists on this point. Rare is the religious-Zionist spokesman who will admit an incompatibility between Judaism and democracy. One sometimes finds, especially among the religious ultra-nationalists statements about the foreign or non-Jewish nature of democracy but they are unusual. This is not true in the *haredi* sector. Although the major *haredi* dailies, *Hamodia* and *Yated Ne'eman* are generally circumspect, *haredi* leaders make no secret of the fact that the principle which Ben-Gurion enunciated so often, that Israel is a state based upon the rule of law and not rule by *halakha*, is an anathema to them. Indeed, rule of law is often mentioned as one of the major shortcomings of the Jewish state. Rabbi Eliezer Menachem Schach is the preeminent leader of one of the two major segments of the *haredi* public. He accuses the secularists of saying:

Let us, the House of Israel be like all the nations, a democratic state, a state of law and not a state of *halakha*, that is, a state with the laws of idol worshippers and not the laws of the Torah.[6]

On the other hand, even those who believe that democracy and Judaism are compatible with one another, cannot reconcile the conception of majority rule at the theoretical level with a Jewish state which is governed in accordance with Jewish law. Authority in a democracy resides with the majority of the population whereas it resides with rabbinical sages in a religious state.[7] The problem, however, is purely hypothetical, not only because such a state is so unlikely to ever be formed but because Jewish law is subject to interpretation by the rabbis. This makes it far more flexible than one might otherwise imagine. It is really impossible to know how the rabbis would dictate where human authority resides if they were confronted with such a question at the practical level.

The real conflict between democracy and Jewish law is not in the realm of legislation by the Knesset or the theoretical mandates of *halakha* but in the role of the Jewish tradition in shaping attitudes and values which serve as preconditions to the functioning of a democratic system. As Nicholas Demerath observes, "despite religion's prominence as a source of political legitimacy and campaign rhetoric, it is rarely a dominant factor in the affairs of state."[8] This is true in Israel as well, but the role of religion in the formation of the political culture of Israeli society and in shaping the political propensities of the religious sector of the population in particular, should not be minimized.[9]

I suggested in the first chapter that a number of attitudes basic to the foundation of a democratic society were incompatible with religious values. These are all true in the case of Judaism and Israel. But the most serious conflict between attitudes necessary for the maintenance of a stable democratic society in Israel and attitudes fostered by high religious commitment has to do with the rights of Arabs. Judaism in Israel has become increasingly particularistic and ethnocentric. It promotes little tolerance for the individual rights of non-Jewish citizens, and even less for group rights of minorities. In the mind of most religiously committed Jews, the Arabs represent a danger and a security threat and strong measures, including a denial of their civil rights are justified.[10] I would summarize the dominant tendency as one that grudgingly acknowledges the right of non-Jews to live in Israel, to live their private lives in accordance with their religious or cultural norms but only insofar as this has no influence on other Jews or on the public life of the state. Even this tendency stretches the limits of *halakhic* tolerance, as the *halakha* is understood by many rabbinic sages.

An article in *T'khumin*, the most distinguished annual dealing with matters of Jewish law and public issues from an Orthodox perspective, addressed the question of the status of Moslems in Israel according to Jewish law.[11] The author seems to phrase himself carefully and there is no trace of polemic in the tone of the article, a fact that makes the conclusions all the more disturbing. According to the writer, under the ideal conditions envisioned by Jewish law, non-Jews in the Land of Israel should live in servitude to Jews. In fact, their very right to live in the Land of Israel is problematic. A Jew is permitted though not required to save non-Jews if their lives are in danger. However, non-Jews should not to benefit from free public services. These are basic principles, the author stresses, according to which a Jewish society ought to be constructed. The *halakhic* imperative to subjugate non-Jews living under Jewish rule may be relaxed because of political constraints, but Jews should never lose sight of the ideal society to which they should aspire. (It is only fair to add that the editor of the volume challenged the author's understanding of *halakha* in a brief note at the conclusion of the article.)

Universalism, a central component in the American Jewish understanding of Judaism, one that extends to many Orthodox as well, is deliberately rejected by mainstream Orthodoxy in Israel. The signs of Jewish particularism are quite noticeable. Everything is perceived from within a Jewish prism and judged from within a Jewish perspective. And the rise of particularism has implications for the interpretation of morality as well. Religious Jews in Israel have redefined the very term "morality" in particularistic rather than universalistic terms. According to the rabbi who pioneered the establishment of extremist education within the religious-Zionist school system, Jews are enjoined to maintain themselves in isolation from other peoples. Foreign culture is a particular anathema when its standards are used to criticize Jews.[12] There is no place in Judaism for "a humanistic attitude in determining responses to hostile behavior of the Arab population" says one of them.[13]

These attitudes and values derive from a religious perspective. Behind them lies a world-view which is formed, in part, by basic *halakhic* notions that divide the world into right and wrong, good and evil, pure and impure. True, these attitudes and values do not carry the force of *halakhic* norms. They don't obligate anybody to observe them or follow them. Indeed, they are rarely articulated. They are conveyed by indirection and in a matter of fact manner, as basic assumptions not only of Judaism but of human nature and the cosmos. But for that very reason, they are more difficult to challenge and are more readily dispersed among population groups — especially poorly educated Jews from Islamic countries who are not punctilious in observing *halakhic* norms but who do internalize many presuppositions of the religious tradition as they are conveyed by the present religious elite.

This parallels Hava Lazrus-Yafeh's observation that there is a basic Islamic orientation which, in denying that man is ever the measure of things "engendered a general mood, never a clearly defined political theory."[14] Similarly, deep suspicion of the non-Jew, the conviction that the non-Jew seeks to totally destroy all Jews, is deeply embedded in the religious culture. Not every religious Jew shares that belief. On the other hand, precisely because it is not articulated in specific *halakhic* norms or asserted as a tenet of Jewish faith or formulated as an empirically testable statement, it possesses a mythic power to persuade without being easily refuted. Both the Holocaust, the enmity of the Arab states toward Israel, Arab terrorism against Jews and the applause or even the failure of Arab leaders to condemn such attacks nourishes this suspicion and renders it plausible to non-religious Israelis, especially but not exclusively those of more limited educational background. The difference between the religious and non-religious sectors of the population, however, is that the suspicion and hostility is not only more wide-spread among the former but it receives specific theological sanction. Thus, for example, according to one *haredi* writer:

The Arab world that torments us is that which concludes the list of kingdoms that are destined to hinder Israel in its path in exile ... and the righteous messiah, whose coming we await, will overcome and conquer them.[15]

or

The wars of Satan — in the image of Egypt and Syria and other satanic figures — [is] a war to totally uproot the essence of the Jew from all generations ...[16]

An editorial in *Niv Hamoreh*, the journal of the association of *haredi* teachers devoted a lengthy article explaining Arab hostility in general and the Yom Kippur war in particular. The essay explained that whereas wars between gentiles are fought for material reasons, their wars against Israel are always wars between profanity and holiness. "Hatred of the world for the nation of eternity" is the reality. The gentile nations and the Jews "are two types of entities, which contradict each other like fire and water ..." Since the "refugees of European Jewry have gathered in the Land of Israel", the Land of Israel is now the focus of the gentiles' hostility. The Arabs are not seeking land but rather the destruction of all Jews.[17]

Having converted Arab hostility to Jews and Israel into a matter of theological and even cosmic significance, distinctions between Arab states, or between Arabs living within Israel and other Arabs are necessarily blurred. Indeed, the assertion of such distinctions would undermine the mythic construct. Hence, it is not surprising that religious Jews who constitute the primary audience for these and similar articles, exhibit greater hostility or suspicion of all Arabs, including those within the borders of Israel, or that they are relatively more amenable to proposals that would deny them basic civil and political rights.

Not all religious leaders understand Judaism and its imperatives in the manner described so far. Talmudic masters, heads of one of the most prominent *yeshivot* (school for advanced

Talmudic study) in Israel, Rabbis Yehuda Amital and Aharon Lichtenstein argue for a very different interpretation of the tradition — one that places emphasis on the essential equality of all people since all are created in the image of God. Their theological perspective has not only led them to insist upon the equal treatment of Arabs and Jews within Israel but has led them to adopt positions on Arab-Israel relations that are far more accommodating than those of the National Religious Party from whose ranks they seceded. In addition, a large minority who define themselves as *dati* and are committed to observance of Torah would grant Israeli Arabs equality. A recent survey of attitudes toward Arab rights in Israel among all Israeli Jews offered respondents three alternative choices on their attitudes toward Arab rights in Israel. The first choice was that only Jews have rights, the second choice was that only Jews have national rights but Arabs have individual rights and the third choice was that both nations have individual as well as national rights. Among the general population, 62 percent chose option two or three; 26 percent chose the third option, i.e. they were prepared to grant Arabs national as well as individual rights. Among those who defined themselves as *dati*, 44 percent chose the second or third option, 13 percent choosing the national rights alternative. Among those who defined themselves as *haredim*, 24 percent were prepared to grant individual rights to Arabs and 8 percent were even prepared to grant them national rights.[18]

RELIGIOUS CHANGES IN ISRAELI LIFE

This chapter has argued that among religious Jews in general and their leaders in particular, one finds tendencies inimicable to democracy and these tendencies stem less from the imperatives of *halakha* than from assumptions, moods, and a general orientation present within the religious public. But moods, atti-

tudes and even general orientations are amenable to development and change without having to overcome legalistic hurdles.
Indeed attitudes and values concerning the Jewish tradition
have undergone dramatic change as I have tried to show elsewhere.[19] Regardless of how one evaluates the weight of the
Jewish tradition, it is not one sided. The option of interpretation
in a more liberal, humanitarian, universalist vein, more compatible with the maintenance of stable democratic structures, exists.
The question, therefore, is why this interpretation is virtually
though not entirely absent in *dati* circles in Israel? Why has
Judaism in Israel undergone a transformation in the direction of
particularism and ethnocentrism rather than moralism, universalism, and political liberalism — in other words why has Israeli
Judaism become less rather than more compatible with the preconditions for a stable democratic society?

There are a number of answers to this question — historical,
sociological and political. The most obvious factor is that when
religious Jews, leaders as well as masses, express that which we
define as anti-democratic values, it is not democracy which they
see as the critical issue. They are not acting out anti-democratic
scenarios in any deliberate fashion. Unlike fascists, for example,
even the most particularist and authoritarian *dati* spokesmen do
not view their behavior or ideology as opposition to democracy.
Democratic values and norms are simply not a referent. These
leaders believe they are behaving in accordance with the precepts
of Judaism, but more specifically they are acting to strengthen the
security and well being of the Jewish people. *Haredi* Jews not
only believe they are better Jews because they are more pious,
devout, and religiously observant; they are also convinced that
they care more than anyone else for other Jews. The *haredi* press
delights in drawing invidious comparisons between *haredim* who
care for Jews, and the Israeli left wing which they charge is concerned only for the rights of Arabs. Among religious-Zionists of all
stripes — not only the ultra-nationalist settlers of the occupied
territories who are not necessarily the most anti-democratic in

attitudes — there is a firm belief that they are the better Zionists and that the values and ideals which they espouse are, with the exception of the desire to impose religious law, totally consistent with the values and ideals of the Zionist pioneers whom they hold in the greatest esteem. As we shall see, they are correct. In other words, attitudes and values which the observer labels anti-democratic and threatening to social order, freedom of choice, and basic human decency, are viewed by many if not a majority of *datiim* as part of the struggle for Jewish security and well being. Meir Kahane was no hero in most *dati* circles, but many of them believed that his basic error was in the fact that he was too zealous on behalf of ideals which all Jews share or at least ought to share. Many *datiim*, and according to some surveys, a majority of *dati* youth, identified with his values. That is the difference between attitudes toward Kahane and attitudes toward a figure such as Knesset member Yosi Sarid (who is a special focus of hatred) or the Citizens Rights Movement. Kahane, they will tell you, may have gone too far, but he went too far in a proper cause. The Zionist left has gone too far in the wrong cause.

Another explanation for changes in religious attitudes toward democracy in general and the rights of the Arab minority in Israel in particular must be understood in light of changes that have taken place within Israeli society in general. Religious spokesman need no longer concern themselves with secular alternatives to the religious tradition. They need no longer respond to alternate conceptions of Judaism that stress univer-salist or ethical components within that tradition because secular Judaism no longer poses an ideology which competes with religious Judaism.[20] Therefore, those most capable of leading the battle against the competition, politicians, but espe-cially religious intellectuals, find that their influence has declined and the balance of authority within the religious world has shifted in favor of the rabbinical elite, who by virtue of their narrow training, career opportunities, and significant referents, tend to be more particularistic and xenophobic.

The Jewish tradition, which the rabbis insist is theirs alone to interpret, is not, as we noted, the same tradition over which they held sway in the past. The transformation of the tradition has taken place independently of the influence of the rabbinical elite. The tradition has been nationalized, among both non-religious as well as religious-Zionists, through a selective interpretation of sacred texts and of Jewish history. Emphasis is given to the sanctity and centrality of *eretz yisrael*, the Land of Israel. In the past, Zionists celebrated their radical departure from the Jewish tradition in their efforts to reclaim and settle the Land. Today, Israelis celebrate their continuity with the tradition in this regard. What is all the more remarkable is that *eretz yisrael* has come to symbolize both loyalty to the State of Israel as well as loyalty to Judaism. Baruch Kimmerling points out that the term *eretz yisrael* has increasingly replaced the term State of Israel in the pronouncements of national leaders, especially those on the political right.[21] To be a good Jew means to live in the Land of Israel under conditions of Jewish autonomy.

RELIGION AND SOCIAL ORDER

The foregoing discussion suggests that religion plays a major role in shaping the values of Israeli Jews — values that for better or for worse instill a sense of loyalty and commitment to the larger collective. Not surprisingly, these and other values associated with the religious tradition are most strongly internalized by Jews who are closest to the religious tradition and least strongly internalized, even rejected by some of those most distant from the tradition. A recent study of religious attitudes and beliefs among Israeli Jews, the most comprehensive study of this nature ever undertaken in Israel, reenforces this view.[22] Respondents were divided into four categories. The categories and the percent of Jews who identified with each of them were: "strictly observant"

(14 percent), "observant to a great extent" (24 percent), "somewhat observant" (41 percent) and "totally non-observant" (21 percent). Respondents' religious beliefs and observance of religious injunctions corresponded to their own self- definition. There is a linear correlation between religious attitudes and identification with the Jewish people and with Zionism. Among the "strictly observant" and those who are "observant to a great extent", over 80 percent answered definitely yes to the question of whether they feel part of the Jewish people throughout the world. Sixty one percent of the "somewhat observant" felt that way but only 46 percent of the "totally non-observant" gave that response. Sixty and 61 percent of the "totally observant" and the "observant to a great extent" answered that they definitely consider themselves Zionists. This is true of 45 percent of those who are "somewhat observant" and only 40 percent of those who are "totally non-observant".

Another set of questions demonstrated the correlation between religion and values which promote social order on the one hand and the negative correlation between religion and values of individual autonomy. Respondents were presented with a list of values and asked which if any of them they find to be very important or important as guiding principles in their lives. As we would expect, the greater the level of observance the greater the importance attributed to the value of living in Israel or feeling part of the Jewish people. But there is also a relationship between religious observance and other values.

There are two values which become more important as respondents become less observant. These are: "enjoying beauty in one's life" and behaving according to one's feelings." The values which are negatively correlated with religious observance are: telling the truth, contributing to charity, raising a family, honoring one's parents and engaging in voluntary community work.

There is one value, not mentioned yet, in which the two extreme groups deviate in the same direction from the majority of Israelis. Both the "totally non-observant" and the "strictly observant" are far less likely to view army service as a very important principle in their lives. The obvious explanation is that the *haredim* among the "strictly observant" abjure army service, whereas the "totally non-observant" are more concerned with self and less committed to the collective national value. Finally, there is one value in which the "strictly observant" alone deviate. They are far less likely to list "having a good time" as a guiding principle in their lives.

SUMMARY

The data are troubling because they suggest the important contribution which religion makes to the internalization of social virtues and civil responsibility but how inimicable religion is to individual freedoms and interreligious (or inter-ethnic) harmony. I don't believe there are any easy solutions to the problem. To one who is committed to both religion and democracy, to both the Jewish tradition and Arab-Jewish harmony the only answer is to exert one's influence in favor of balancing the tensions. One tries to assess the direction in which the pendulum is pointing or where the balance is shifting and then seek the appropriate correction. In addition, it suggests to me that while there is no perfect accommodation, the resolution begins by a recognition of the problem and by the sense of both advocates of religion and advocates of democracy that each has a stake in how the other defines the conditions necessary for a well ordered society.

ENDNOTES

1. Part of the material in this chapter originally appeared in somewhat different form in my article, "Attitudes Toward Democracy Among Israeli Religious

Leaders," Edy Kaufman and Shukri Abed (eds.), *Democracy, Peace and the Israeli-Palestinian Conflict* (Boulder: Lynne Rienner, 1993), pp. 135–161.

2. For a summary of the most important studies in this regard see Yochanan Peres and Ephraim Yuchtman-Yaar, *Trends in Israeli Democracy: The Public's View* (Boulder: Lynne Rienner, 1992) and Yochanan Peres, *Religious Adherence and Political Attitudes* (Ramat-Gan: Sociological Institute for Community Studies, Bar-Ilan University, Sociological Papers, 1 October, 1992).

3. Some laws and administrative regulations discriminate against Arabs and the present government has addressed them. But even in the past, discrimination against Arabs, like pre-1960 discrimination against Blacks in the United States, was challenged in the name of the societies own higher values.

4. See David Kretzmer, *The Legal Status of the Arabs in Israel* (Boulder: Westview Press, 1990).

5. The late Rabbi Meir Kahane, though not a renowned rabbinical scholar, nevertheless anchored himself in rabbinic text and certainly represented one stream within the Jewish tradition. According to Kahane:

The liberal west speaks about the rule of democracy, of the authority of the majority, while Judaism speaks of the Divine truth that is immutable and not subject to the ballot box or to majority error. The liberal west speaks about the absolute equality of all people while Judaism speaks of spiritual *status*, of the choseness of the Jew from above all other people, of the special and exclusive relationship between G-d and Israel." (Meir Kahane, *Uncomfortable Questions For Comfortable Jews* (Secaucus, N.J.: Lyle Stuart, 1987), p. 159).

Other rabbis, less politically extreme than Kahane, express opinions that range along a wide spectrum. Zvi Weinman, writes that even if all the Knesset members were religiously observant Jews, the democratic system is tainted because it can in theory decide matters contrary to the Torah. (Zvi Weinman, "Religious Legislation — A Negative View, "*T'khumin*, vol. VII, in Hebrew, 1986, p. 521).

A more subtle objection to democracy is contained in the notion that belief in the equality of all men undermines the notion of God as king. As is seen in the following quotation, there is no direct objection to democracy, but the observation concerning the consequences of democracy implies a negative evaluation.

In contemporary democratic society there are no kings and there are no counts. The relationship toward the elected officials is only as "the first among equals" and the sense of elevation and self abnegation is absent ... And since human beings are proud and filled with the sense of equality and their own self importance, it is difficult for them to accustom themselves to the idea that there is after all a King above them, for whom their importance is as nothing and whom they are obliged to serve as slaves. And in the absence of a wish to feel enslaved, humans are swept, in their desire for self justification, to a denial of the existence of the King. (Rabbi Moshe Rubinstein, "Causes for the

Undermining of Faith in the Modern World," *Diglenu* (Nisan, 1981, in Hebrew), p. 16).

On the other hand, according to another distinguished rabbi, "the democratic approach, whose substance is consideration for the will of the people, their demands and their needs, is among the foundation stones of Israeli *halakha*." (Nathan Zvi Friedman, "Notes on Democracy and *Halakha*," *T'khumin*, vol. IV, in Hebrew, 1984 p. 255).

Eliezer Schweid concludes his discussion of Rabbi Chaim Hirshenson's ideas about a democratic state according to *halakha* with the observation that "the political system that the Torah intended is democratic in its basis". (Eliezer Schweid, *Democracy and Halakha: Reflections on the Teachings of Rabbi Chaim Hirshenson* (Jerusalem: Magnes Press, in Hebrew, 1978), p. 75).

Finally, to Rabbi Sol Roth "it is clear that the fundamental principles of democracy, namely, representative government and rule by majority, inhere in a Jewish tradition." (*Halakha and Politics: The Jewish Idea of a State* (New York: Ktav, 1988), p. 141).

6. Elazar Menachem Man Schach, *Sefer Mikhtavim V'Ma'amarim* (Bnei Brak: n.p. 1988), pp. 6–7. The citation is from a letter written in the summer of 1977 in the wake of the electoral victory of the Likud. The purpose of the letter is to assure Rav Schach's corespondent that nothing has changed.

7. This is the thrust of an article by Rabbi Haim David Halevy, "Majority and Minority in a Democratic Jewish State," Department of Torah Culture, Ministry of Education and Culture, *Yahadut V'Demokratia* (Jerusalem: Department of Torah Culture, Ministry of Education and Culture, in Hebrew, 1989), pp. 29–40.

8. N.J. Demerath III, "Religious Capital and Capital Religions: Cross-Cultural and Non-Legal Factors in the Separation of Church and State," *Daedalus*, 120 (Summer, 1991), p. 38.

9. The possibility that religion may exercise great political efficacy by influencing the religious culture without necessarily possessing great structural or institutional influence is developed, at the theoretical level in Nicholas J. Demerath III and Rhys H. Williams, "Religion and Power in the American Experience," Thomas Robbins and Dick Anthony, *In Gods We Trust: New Patterns of Religious Pluralism in America*. New Brunswick, N.J.: Transaction Books, second edition, revised and expanded, 1991), pp. 427–448.

10. Religion acts independently of education and ethnicity in the formation of Jewish attitudes toward Arabs. The religious Jew is more likely to harbor prejudice and less likely to respect the political rights of Arabs. Ephraim Yuchtman-Yaar, "The Israeli Public and the Intifada: Attitude Change or Entrenchment?," Ehud Sprinzak and Larry Diamond (eds.) *Israeli Democracy Under Stress: Cultural and Institutional Perspectives* (Boulder: Lynne Rienner, 1993) provides additional documentation to a phenomenon which is supported by every survey of Israeli public opinion with which I am familiar.

11. Elisha Aviner, "The Status of Ishmaelites in the State of Israel According to *Halakha*," *T'khumin*, in Hebrew, 8 (1987), pp. 337–359.

12. Cited in Charles S. Liebman, "Jewish Ultra-Nationalism in Israel, William Frankel (ed.), *Survey of Jewish Affairs 1985.* (London: Associated University Presses, 1985), p. 46.
13. *Ibid.*
14. Hava Lazrus-Yafeh, "Political Traditions and Responses in Islam," Israel Academy of Sciences and Humanities, *Totalitarian Democracy and After* (Jerusalem: The Magnes Press, 1984), p. 131.
15. Aryei Rosen, "In the Fury of Days of Fire and Blood," *Diglenu* (Heshvan, 1973), p. 4.
16. Simha Elberg, "The Yom Kippur War," *Diglenu* (Adar, 1974), p. 3.
17. "On the Agenda," [this is the regular title of the editorial], *Niv Hamoreh*, no. 46 (Kislev, 1973), pp. 3, 17.
18. Peres, *op. cit.*, p. 30.
19. Charles S. Liebman, *Attitudes Toward Jewish-Gentile Relations in the Jewish Tradition and Contemporary Israel*, Kaplan Centre, University of Cape Town, Occasional Papers, 1984; and Charles S. Liebman and Steven M. Cohen, *Two Worlds of Judaism: The Jewish Experience in Israel and the United States* (New Haven: Yale University Press, 1990).
20. Yisrael Segal, a senior editor for Israeli television, was raised in a *haredi* home and became a secularist of anti-religious leanings. He reports about the experience of a young *haredi* who came to him for help in escaping the *haredi* world. (Yisrael Segal, "An Adopted Son of God," *Politika*, no. 41 ((November, 1991, in Hebrew)), pp. 43–45). The effort to escape failed and Segal notes the basic problem.

    Whereas in the first generation of those who abandoned religion … the Zionist vision awaited at the threshold, and whereas at the time of the [Zionist] pioneers who left the path of religion, a faith in Marxism and a dream of paradise on earth [could provide a substitute] … in Israel of the 90's what awaits one who leaves [religion] is a world devoid of absolute values: a difficult daily struggle with a grey, complex often tortured reality. (p. 45).

21. Baruch Kimmerling, "Between the Primordial and the Civil Definition of the Collective Identity: *Eretz Israel* or the State of Israel?", Erik Cohen, Moshe Lissak and Uri Almagor (eds.), *Comparative Social Dynamics: Essays in Honor of S.N. Eisenstadt* (Boulder: Westview Press, 1985), pp. 262–83.
22. Shlomit Levy, Hanna Levinsohn and Elihu Katz, *Beliefs, Observances and Social Interaction Among Israeli Jews* (Jerusalem: The Louis Guttman Israel Institute of Applied Social Research, 1993).

FIVE

Religion, Modernization and the Peace Process in Israel

It was observed, in the previous chapter, that the influence of religion is experienced most directly by Jews who are most observant of religious injunctions. This chapter points out that religion has an impact on almost all Israeli Jews and Israeli political institutions. This impact, so much more pronounced than is found in any other western industrial democracy, is best explained by the peculiar security conditions which Israel has confronted since its establishment. This was alluded to in the previous chapter but it merits more elaborate explanation.

Israelis view their society and their state as Jewish, and wish it to remain Jewish, and because efforts to formulate secular Judaism in conceptual not to mention ritual terms no longer attracts more than a small number of Israelis, the vast majority resonate to the perception of their condition, their problems and their future in the rhetoric and symbols of the religious tradition. As Baruch Kimmerling, the sociologist who is himself an ardent secularist has noted:

There are secular individuals, groups and even sub-cultures in Israel. Their daily behavior and their own identity is secular. There are even those who wage a cultural or religious war against this or that aspect of state efforts to impose this or that religious practice or *halakhic* norm on the general public or on one segment of that public. But when the vast majority of Israeli Jews refer to their collective national identity, that identity is defined for the most part by concepts, values, symbols and collective memory that is anchored primarily in the Jewish religion. In other words, there are secular Jews in the world and in Israel, but there is grave doubt if there is such a thing as secular Judaism.[1]

Kimmerling may exaggerate. There still are some Jews who believe in secular Judaism. The difference is that whereas they were once found in large numbers among the founders and leaders of the state, individuals who were prominent in political and cultural life, their numbers have been severely reduced. As Hanna Herzog writes in her description of a recent political campaign in Israel:

The more Jewish terms the secular people could use to define and perceive them-selves, the less alienated they felt from the Orthodox. Jewish tradition became a source of legitimization for the political claims of all the parties — each of which endowed it with its own meaning.[2]

At least since the 1960's and until most recently, the Jewish tradition engendered a broad consensus among Israeli Jews offering a common set of symbols, a common language of public discourse, and the sense of an integrated social order. The central values of this tradition, as far as the vast majority of Israelis were concerned were Jewish peoplehood and what Asher Arian, Ilan Talmud and Tamar Hermann call "the religion of security".[3]

According to these authors, the security threat has been a permanent condition of life, and requires more than a "rational and professional" response which the Israeli Defense Forces (IDF), Israeli intelligence and the General Security Services provide. The authors argue that there is a symbolic and psycho-logical dimension to Israel's security threat. Israelis meet the threat at the psychological and symbolic level through belief in the Almighty and the Jewish people.[4]

Basing their conclusions on questionnaire responses from a representative sample of Israeli Jewish adults conducted in 1986 the authors demonstrate the interrelationship between the values of Jewish peoplehood and security.

The notion of a hostile world is deeply embedded in the Jewish tradition and the "impression that the world was basi-cally hostile and often anti-semitic ... characterized the way the Israeli public viewed national security policy."[5] According to the authors, even mainstream Zionist parties analyze the conflict between Israel and Arabs "in the spirit and often in the lexicon of the persecution suffered by Jews in most European countries and some of the countries of the Muslim world."[6]

Accompanying the sense of security threat is a high level of certainty that Israel will prevail despite Gentile hostility and antisemitism. "Israel must trust in the guardian of Israel", and "the guardian of Israel will prevail", Israelis affirm. This core value, the authors note:

> is related to religious belief, but the religious have no monopoly on it. It is to be found more often among those who support the right but supporters of the left also share the belief... It permeates the society and legitimates behavior and policy.[7]

Israelis disagree as to who or what is represented in the referent "guardian". Most Israelis think it refers to the IDF, some to God, some to the people of Israel and some to the State of Israel. It is not only the language of this core belief that is religious (the term Guardian is a synonym for God in the Jewish tradition), but as Arian and his associates point out, the conviction that some entity must be trusted and will prevail is at its core an extra-rational belief. Hence, disagreement over the referent to the term "guardian" doesn't prevent the development of broad consensus and a common language of discourse.

My argument is that Israeli concerns over security are related to Israeli commitment to the Jewish tradition. By tradition I refer to the sense of Jewish continuity, Jewish history and the central myths of Judaism which evoke a sense of identity and commitment among the vast majority of Israelis. Tradition, understood in this broader sense, reinforces concerns over security, and concerns over security reinforces commitment to tradition which, in turn, supports the pattern of ritual behavior and religious belief among Israeli Jews. For the majority of Israeli Jews, those from Sephardic background in particular, the tradition's conception of the Jewish condition in the world (the classical metaphor, "a lamb among seventy wolves" suggests the flavor of the conception), provides some explanation for Arab enmity toward Israel.[8] The classical Zionist expectation of normal relationships between Jews and non-Jews once Jews have obtained independent statehood, appears to lack a foundation in reality. While developments in the past year or two may raise reservations in the minds of many Israeli Jews about the traditional religious paradigm of Jewish-Gentile relations, a point that may be crucial in predicting future developments, it certainly seemed credible up until then.

The tradition socializes the Jew to the expectation of security threats, and security threats serve to strengthen the Jews' commitment to the tradition. It is helpful, in this regard, to recall Ronald Inglehart's analysis in his book *Culture Shifts in Advanced Industrial Societies*.[9] "Vulnerability", to use Inglehart's term, promotes the "need for a sense of security, which religion and absolute cultural norms have traditionally provided."[10] Inglehart attributes the decline of traditional religious social and sexual norms in advanced industrial society to the increasing sense of security which the population enjoys. One doesn't need, he says, the security of the absolute, rigid rules that religious sanctions can provide. The belief which Israelis Jews share that their physical security is threatened would strengthen rather than weaken their need for absolute cultural norms.

The second reason, according to Inglehart, that societal and religious norms are more important to those who feel vulnerable has to do with the function these norms perform. Without such norms, Inglehart observes, "a society would tend to tear itself apart".[11] Religious norms such as "honor thy father and mother", he says, are linked to maintaining the family unity which, he believes, is less crucial than it once was with the rise of the welfare state. It remains crucial, I would add, when one feels a sense of physical vulnerability. Family, as the Israeli army itself believes, is absolutely critical in maintaining the morale of the soldier and in providing him, and virtually all Israeli Jews, with a support system for their fears.[12]

This sense of the importance of the immediate family and then, by extension, the broader community of Israeli Jews (i.e. the extended family), is further strengthened by the nature of the threat which Israelis face. The threat to their survival stems from the fact of their Jewishness and can only be met through the collective effort of Jews. An individual may be able to overcome the threat to his material welfare through his own initiative; indeed, he may be better able to do so by acting alone. An individual may also feel that challenges to his mental or physical health can only be met through his own initiative. But threats to the physical safety of Israeli Jews can only be confronted through collective activity. The strength, security and well being of the individual Jew in Israel rests primarily on the strength, security and well being of the larger community.

In the case of security threats of the kind Israel faces, particularly in times of relative peace, perception is no less important than reality. Indeed, perception, to a great extent (though not entirely) dictates policy which in turn interacts with reality. As the political anthropologist Myron Aronoff notes, that which fundamentally divides Israeli Jews is "their evaluation of whether or not the Jewish people and its state are capable of being 'normal' and whether or not such a condition (if it is possible) is one that should be sought".[13] He goes on to observe that "these orientations are related to different perceptions of security, perceptions of 'the other' and temporal perception of myth and history".[14] It is a small minority who is likely to perceive the Israeli condition as secure and to see history as linear.

This minority constitutes that segment of Israeli society which defines its behavior as totally non-observant. Its values were described in the previous chapter. As I noted, it is the least nationalistic — both in terms of its sense of Jewish peoplehood and Zionism.

But one cannot consign this group and the values it espouses to the status of an insignificant minority. First of all, the pervasive nature of the secular, individualistic, consumption oriented values in western society suggests that all Israelis, even the more observant will have internalized some of them to some degree. So the set of values which provide an alternative to the tradition are certainly present, although the pervasive sense of threat to security which Arian, Talmud and Hermann document, help us to understand why the tradition has withstood the challenge for so long. In addition, the totally non-observant are an influential and I suspect a growing minority. Among those Israelis whose fathers were born in the west (according to the Guttman Report referred to in the previous chapter), 48 percent were totally non-observant. Among those with a full college education 40 percent describe themselves as totally non-observant.

This minority is obviously an influential one. I have little doubt that it includes a grossly disproportionate share of journalists and political commentators, academics (faculty from the social sciences and humanities in particular), and the top echelon of the governmental and business bureaucracy. This is the "new class" as social scientists increasingly refer to them. This "new class" is distinguished from the older middle and upper middle class by its professional expertise, its creation of social symbols and its control of information rather than ownership of property.

The totally non-observant compromise that segment of the Israeli public least attracted by and most disdainful of the Jewish concepts, symbols, values, norms and collective memory of Judaism and the Jewish people. It is not surprising if we were to find that it is the very segment of the public most engaged in occupations (the media, academics, senior bureaucrats, industrial leaders) whose very foundation is universalist in orientation and which relies most heavily upon universalist rather than Jewishly particular associations. These are the same groups which offer the strongest support to the peace process. It was from within their ranks that the technocrats who drafted the first Israeli-PLO accords were drawn. Michael Keren characterizes them as "a knowledge-power nexus, dominated by [foreign minister] Peres and his allies among Israel's professionals, who had little concern for cognitive changes [among the Jews and Palestinians]."[15]

The late Christopher Lasch describes this same type of elite in the United States.[16] Members of the elite, he says, have mounted a crusade, "to extend the range of personal choice in matters where most people feel the need for solid moral guidelines". The majority of society appears:

to the makers of educated opinion [as] hopelessly dowdy, unfashionable, and provincial ... the new elites regard the masses with mingled scorn and apprehension.[17]

Lasch argues that the loyalties of this elite are international rather than national. What is true of the Israeli elite, especially the academics and intellectuals whom I know, is that their significant reference groups are colleagues and peers in the west. It is the intellectual elite of the west who shape the world views and value preferences of Israeli intellectuals. Their political loyalties may be Israeli but their cultural affinities are not Israeli and least of all, Jewish.

The success of this elite, and the increased penetration of western consumer oriented individualistic values in Israel is evident in the growing dissolution of Israeli civil religion. In other words, the evocative power of the symbols rituals and myths, which emerged out of the Zionist movement and which called upon the Jewish citizenry to sacrifice their individual preferences and private needs for those of the civil or social order has been severely weakened.

The evidence for the decline of civil religion, in the absence of survey research data is admittedly partial and impressionistic.

The Israeli media has provided extensive publicity in the last few years to studies that question the stature, the heroism, and the motivation of Israel's early heroes. Television dramas have been written in the same skeptical vein. They have occasioned some dissent but their publication in the press and their airing on public TV suggests that Israeli society is far less sensitive than it once was to debunking the civil religion's mythical heroes.[18]

Israel's willingness to enter into a peace agreement with the Palestinians is attributable at least in part, to a recognition by the political and military elite that Israel has already been over-taken by the demand for individual autonomy, a demand that erodes if not shatters any ideological or symbolic system which provides a society with meaning. As the IDF Chief of Staff Amnon Shahak, commenting on the rise in the number of young Israelis who consider military service "inappropriate for them" noted: the problem is "a preference for individualism over the collective in an age of liberalism".[19]

This became very clear in the reaction, as recorded by television reporters, of Israeli soldiers to their departure from the Gaza strip. As Orit Shochat notes, in her survey of media coverage, a young officer is quoted as saying: "I want to get out already, and that's that". And she goes on to point out that what the soldiers want is "to go home, in the original meaning of the term. They want easier conditions". Perhaps at home, she goes on to note, they may even have a family car with a bumper sticker protesting any surrender of territory.[20]

Other signs of the decline of the civil religion include the transformation of civil religious celebrations into private events. A good example is the decline of Independence Day as a major holiday and the transfer of celebrations from massive events to family barbecues in public parks.[21]

Recent election campaigns including the 1994 Federation of Labor (Histadrut) elections is another example. Traditional party leaders were defeated in these elections and replaced by younger, more glamorous candidates whose election campaigns focused on the individual voter and on the fulfillment of the voter's needs rather than societal or collective needs.

It is not without irony that today, the sector most committed to the values of Israeli civil religion is the religious-Zionist public which has transformed traditional religion, as I suggested in the last chapter, and doesn't require civil religious symbols, ceremonials, or myths to internalize civil religious values. No one questions that religious-Zionists are to be found, in disproportionate numbers, fulfilling positions such as combat soldiers and officers in the army, where self-sacrifice is still recognized as a virtue.

It is no surprise, therefore, that despite the relatively high levels of traditional observance among Israeli Jews, there are increasing tensions between the more religiously traditional and less religiously traditional segments of the population. The values of adherence or deference to the Jewish tradition on the one hand and modernity, secularism and individual autonomy on the other were always present in Israeli society. Israel avoided a culture war because both the vast majority of Israelis affirmed both these values. Confronted with the dual pressures of security needs and the values they engender on the one hand, and modern consumer oriented values on the other, most Israelis internalized both sets of values. The tensions existed in the hearts and minds of the vast majority of Israelis rather than separating one Israeli Jew from another. But the values of the tradition were already in retreat and should security threats be perceived as less ominous, the retreat is likely to accelerate.

LOOKING AHEAD

If, as was argued here, the "religion of security" is tied to Jewish traditionalism than a decline in one must lead to a decline in the other. Lower levels of traditionalism may, in turn, contribute, to diminished perceptions of security threats. This will happen because security threats are less likely to be perceived through the lenses of Jewish destiny and fate and thereby appear more remote and less ominous. Alternately, loss of traditional faith may mean loss of optimism about the capacity of

Israel to survive the threats that it faces, and hence a greater willingness to compromise and surrender.

If security threats diminish, or if the perception of such threats diminish, it will influence Israeli attitudes toward the religious tradition. If Israeli Jews no longer perceive their collective security as tenuous, if they believe that their society no longer exists under siege, then the package of values which presently characterizes Israeli society — tradition as the cement for national consensus and order, the primacy of collective as opposed to individual welfare, identification with the Jewish people, family as the core institution which protects as well as comforts the individual — is bound to unravel.

Should this occur the way would be opened for the more radical secularists to pursue an agenda item that they have, heretofore, been obliged to defer — the separation of religion and state in the first instance and ultimately, the dejudaization of Israel. At the present time, the vast majority of Israelis, including some who define themselves as "fully observant" are unhappy with many of the provisions of Israeli law which impose religious restrictions on public life. For example, according to the Guttman Report discussed in the last chapter, 67 percent of Israeli Jews support opening of movie theaters and 64 percent favor public transportation on Shabbat, 51 percent favor instituting civil marriage in Israel. But this is not the same as separating religion from state. According to the Guttman Report, 33 percent of Israeli Jews feel that public life in Israel should be less religious than it is, 51 percent feel that it should be just as it is and 16 percent feel it should be more religious. In other words, two-thirds of Israelis are either satisfied with the present status of religion in public life or would like more religion. Even among the one-third who want less religion in public life, most want Israel to remain a Jewish state. The radical secularists find this objectionable. They even want to eliminate the symbolic elements that identify Israel as a Jewish state — its anthem, its flag, its holidays, etc. Among Israeli Arabs, or Palestinians as they prefer to be called, this demand is heard more frequently.

Most of those who oppose any vestige of religion in Israeli public life today are secularists who happen to be Jewish, not "Jewish secularists".[22] They don't seek to interpret Judaism as a national culture. They are simply uninterested in and generally unsympathetic to Judaism. They are prepared to tolerate its presence at the private but not at the public level where they find its prohibitions inconvenient to their styles of life and objectionable to their "modernist" sensitivities. They define democracy in the most libertarian of terms — a system of government which places the individual and not collective goals at the center of its concern, "the expression of man's recognition that all sources of political, social and moral authority inhere in man himself" and that "society and state exist in order to serve the individual ... and are never ends in themselves".[23] They perceive the democratic system as in sharp conflict with Judaism or any religious system of life. In addition, some of them recognize that Israeli Arabs will never become fully integrated into the society or view themselves as anything more than second class citizens as long as Israel retains its Jewish identity. Israeli Arabs who constitute some 17 percent of the population, concur. However, precisely because of Israel's security needs and its tensions with neighboring Arab states, Israeli Arabs, up until the present, were reluctant to press this issue. They feared charges of disloyalty, a charge which is echoed any way in right wing circles. Peace between Israel and the Arab states, even the present agreement between Israel and the PLO, have emboldened Israeli Arabs to openly discuss these concerns[24], a task eased by their Jewish allies who describe themselves as "post Zionists" and who are to be found in substantial numbers in the academy and among the cultural elite.[25]

The development of these tendencies seems almost inevitable. Peace will further legitimate the demands for individual autonomy at the expense of ethnic or national sentiments and the Jewish religion, whose strength rests on its symbolic representation of Jewish ethno-national identity, memories and aspirations will come under increased attack. But the kinds of changes which radical secularists and their allies are likely to favor require new legislation and the organization of political instrumentalities to pursue their goals.

This could play itself out in a variety of scenarios. A decline of Jewish traditionalism and the rise of individualistic values are likely to threaten the social order in Israel just as it is threatening to do in the west. But a weakened social order, weakened consensus, weakened willingness to defer personal needs for collective purposes will be dangerous to Israel's survival assuming, as most observers do, that Arab willingness for peace with Israel is based on their conviction that they can't vanquish it in war. Once the danger becomes manifest, it is likely to spur some kind of counter-cultural affirmation of tradition. I suspect that it will lead to a "modest" realignment of the Israeli political map. "Modest" because whereas the issues which presently structure Israel's political map will change, a similar but not identical alignment is likely to form around the dejudaization issue.

The present party structure of Israel is based on orientations toward security and territory. The right wing consists of those who are deeply suspicious of Arab intentions, those of the Palestinians in particular, and who oppose surrendering territory for promises of peace because of security fears and their emotional attachment to the Land of Israel. They probably comprise a majority, though not an overwhelming majority of Israeli Jews. Consistent with what has been said in this and the preceding chapter, it should come as no surprise to learn that virtually all religious Jews are in the right wing camp. The left wing is comprised of those who are less suspicious of Arab or Palestinian intentions, those who are less emotionally attached to the Land of Israel, and those who find Israeli rule over a recalcitrant Palestinian minority intolerable on moral and/or pragmatic grounds. These will no longer be the issues which exercise the Israeli public. But, in general, with exceptions to be noted, it is the right wing which is most likely to resist dejudaization and the left wing most likely to support it.

The demands to transform the nature of Israeli society is likely to provoke grave resistance among a substantial segment of the Jewish population. Oriental Jews, especially those at the lower income levels will vigorously resist such tendencies. The full integration of Israeli Arabs into the economic life of Israeli society is most likely to result in the displacement and downward mobility of these elements in addition to the offense it brings to their ethnic and religious sentiments. Sephardic Jews will be joined by the older segment of the population including many on the political left. They resent the demands of the religious parties and the attitudes of the religious establishment but their strong Zionist convictions derive, in essence, from their concerns with the welfare of the Jewish people and in many cases their love of the Jewish tradition.[26] They remain Zionists out of conviction that the Jewish state is the natural product of the Jewish tradition and a precondition for Jewish survival. In some respects a Jewish state is more important to them than it is to religious Jews. To the former the state embodies a major dimension of their Judaism. Religious Jews will certainly resist efforts at dejudaization; indeed they are likely to provide the intellectual leadership for the opposition. I suspect that religious-political leaders will moderate the nature of the specifically religious demands they make on the body politic in order to sustain a broad based opposition to dejudaization. In other words, I suspect that the need to preserve the Jewish nature of Israeli society against a threat which is only beginning to be imagined today, will require coalition formation and force religious parties and leaders to compromise specifically religious demands. They may acquiesce to opening of movie theaters or public transportation on the Sabbath since the vast majority of the population favor it. Alternately, as the battle over maintaining a Jewish state intensifies, less observant Jews who favor a Jewish state may moderate their objections to the presence of religion in public life.

Resistance to the dejudaization of Israel is likely to be sharpened by a conviction that security threats only appear to have dissipated, or that those who refuse to express their political convictions in the language of Jewish traditionalism are disloyal and even threatening to the social order. This has already begun to happen. The outcome of the conflict cannot be predicted. It is safer, however, to predict that a bitter fight is likely to precede any resolution.

ENDNOTES

1. Baruch Kimmerling, "Religion, Nationalism and Democracy in Israel," *Zmanim*, nos. 50–51, 13 (Winter, 1994, in Hebrew), p. 129.
2. Hanna Herzog, "Was It On The Agenda: The Hidden Agenda of the 1988 Campaign," Asher Arian and Michal Shamir (eds.), *The Elections In Israel, 1988* (Boulder: Westview Press, 1990), p. 58.
3. Asher Arian, Ilan Talmud, and Tamar Hermann, *National Security and Public Opinion in Israel* (Boulder: Westview Press, published for the Jaffee Center for Strategic Studies, Tel-Aviv University, 1988).
4. *Ibid.*, p. 48.
5. *Ibid.*, p. 80.
6. *Ibid.*, p. 46.
7. *Ibid.*, p. 84.
8. Charles S. Liebman, *Attitudes Toward Jewish-Gentile Relations in the Jewish Tradition and Contemporary Israel* (Kaplan Centre, University of Cape Town, Occasional Papers, 1984).
9. Ronald Inglehart, *Cultural Shifts in Advanced Industrial Society* (Princeton: Princeton University Press, 1990).
10. *Ibid.*, p. 177.
11. *Ibid.*, p. 178.
12. Elihu Katz, Yaacov Trope and Hadassah Haas, "Integration in Army and Nation: An Essay in Institutional Permeability," Erik Cohen, Moshe Lissak and Uri Almagor (eds.), *Comparative Social Dynamics: Essays in Honor of S.N. Eisenstadt* (Boulder: Westview Press, 1985), pp. 315–333.
13. Myron Aronoff, "The Origins of Israeli Political Culture," Ehud Sprinzak and Larry Diamond (eds.), *Israeli Democracy Under Stress* (Boulder: Lynne Rienner, 1993), p. 58.
14. *Ibid.*
15. Michael Keren, "Israeli Professionals and the Peace Process," *Israel Affairs*, 1 (Autumn, 1994), p. 150.
16. Christopher Lasch, "The Revolt of the Elites: Have they canceled their allegiance to America?," *Harper's*, 289 (November, 1974), pp. 39–49. The essay is adapted from a posthumous book *The Revolt of the Elites and the Betrayal of Democracy* (New York: Norton, 1995).

17. *Ibid.*, p. 41.
18. For a summary of debate see the cover story of the *Jerusalem Report*, "Israel's Heroes Under Attacks" December 29, 1994. The lead article by Calev Ben-David, pp. 13–19 is subtitled as follows:

    On stage and screen, in the media and history books, the myths and heroes of Israel and Zionism are being criticized, attacked and reevaluated. Is this the healthy historical revisionism of a changing society, or a growing cynicism that is undermining the country's ideological foundations? (p. 13.)

19. *The New York Times*, (May 31, 1995), p. A10. The quote appears in a feature article by Clyde Haberman titled, "Israel's Army, Once Sacrosanct, Is Now Becoming Deglamourized" which adds evidence to support the thesis of the decline of Israeli civil religion. The army has, heretofore, been its central institution.
20. Orit Shochat, "A Withdrawal That is Too Happy," *Ha'Aretz* (May 20, 1994), p. 12B.
21. Eliezer Don-Yehiya, "Festivals and Political Culture: Independence-Day Celebrations." *The Jerusalem Quarterly*, no. 45. (Winter 1988), pp. 61–84.
22. On the distinction between the types of Jewish secularists see Charles S. Liebman and Steven M. Cohen, *Two Worlds of Judaism: The Jewish Experience in Israel and the United States.* (New Haven: Yale University Press, 1990).
23. Ze'ev Sternhall, "The Battle for Intellectual Control," *Politika*, no. 18, in Hebrew (December, 1987), pp. 2–5.
24. A feature story on the debate whether Israel must change its national anthem and flag because of the sensitivities of its Arab citizens appeared in *The New York Times*, (June 1, 1995), p. 4.
25. Post-Zionist thought is to be found on the pages of two Hebrew language journals, *Teoria U'Bikoret* (Theory and Criticism), published by the Van Leer Institute and more selectively in the pages of *Zmanim* (Times) a publication of Tel-Aviv University's School of History. The controversy assumed more popular dimensions in the summer of 1994 with the publication of an article by the well known Israeli writer Aharon Meged, "The Suicide Wish of the Israeli," *Ha'Aretz* (June 10, 1994). Post-Zionists replied with vigor in the weeks that followed and they were answered, no less vigorously, by their critics. The sense that denuding Israeli of its Jewish character is the primary item on the post-Zionist agenda was articulated by the distinguished historian of modern Israel Anita Shapiro in an interview with her in *Yediot Aharonot's* literary supplement, (December 23, 1994).
26. An expression of this point of view is found in Yehoshua Rash, *Zeh R'ey V'hadesh* (Tel-Aviv: Sifriat Hapoalim, in Hebrew, 1989). This is a collection of articles by politically left wing and secular Zionists who are intensely dedicated to the Jewish tradition. They are associated with Mapam, the most radical of the left wing Zionist parties.

Index

www.ingramcontent.com/pod-product-compliance
Ingram Content Group UK Ltd.
Pitfield, Milton Keynes, MK11 3LW, UK
UKHW020348010325
455677UK00021B/339